BLESS YOU

**Other Discovery House Publishers books
by Warren W. Wiersbe**

Heirs of the King: Living the Beatitudes
The Lost Shepherd: Finding and Keeping the Right Pastor
Who Am I? New Testament Pictures of the Christian Life

BLESS YOU

RECEIVING *and* SHARING THE
BLESSINGS *of the* LORD

WARREN W. WIERSBE

DISCOVERY HOUSE
PUBLISHERS®

Feeding the Soul with the Word of God

Discovery House Publishers is affiliated with RBC Ministries,
Grand Rapids, Michigan.

Discovery House books are distributed to the trade exclusively by
Barbour Publishing, Inc., Uhrichsville, Ohio.

Interior design by Sherri Hoffman

Library of Congress Cataloging-in-Publication Data

Wiersbe, Warren W.
    Bless you : receiving and sharing the blessings of the Lord :
a study of the benedictions of the Bible / Warren W. Wiersbe.
        p. cm.
    ISBN 978-1-57293-235-7
    1. Blessings in the Bible. 2. Benediction. I. Title.
    BS680.B5W54 2008
    220.6—dc22

2008006616

Printed in the United States of America

09 10 11 12 13 / BPI / 9 8 7 6 5 4

Contents

CHAPTER 1

THE GOD WHO BLESSES

I F WE WERE TO REMOVE the words *bless, blessed,* and *blessing* from the Christian vocabulary, our prayer life, congregational worship, and preaching would be greatly affected. These are friendly words that we're accustomed to hearing and using, and life would be barren without them. "Don't say to God, 'Bless the missionaries,'" I heard a veteran missionary say. "Pray for our specific needs," he explained. "Ask God to protect us, provide for us, and help to glorify Jesus. Pray that we don't become discouraged. Pray for laborers to join us in the work."

His words were practical and biblical, but then I remembered that Jacob prayed in general terms when he said, "I will not let you go unless you bless me" (Genesis 32:26). And God answered him. *He gave Jacob a limp!* Perhaps Jacob should have been more specific in his praying. Is a limp a blessing? It can be—at least it was for Jacob. It changed his walk with God and with people—Jacob had frequent difficulties with both—and it helped to make him a God-conquered man. God gave Jacob the new name Israel, which means "he struggled with God and with men and [over-came]" (Genesis 32:27–28). The man with the limp became an overcomer. How strange!

But the life of faith always involves paradoxes. If we want to receive, we must first give. If we want to be leaders, we must first be servants. The way to be exalted is to be humbled, and the way to get a blessing is to be a blessing. When like Jacob we surrender to the Lord, then we can experience His overcoming power. The apostle Paul prayed for divine healing, and God's answer was, "My grace is sufficient for you, for my power is made perfect in weakness" (2 Corinthians 12:9). Paul accepted God's plan and submitted to Him, so he was able to say, "For when I am weak, then I am strong" (2 Corinthians 12:10), another Christian paradox.

In the eternal economy of God, strength that believes itself to be strength is weakness, but weakness that believes itself to be weakness is strength. Weakness plus faith plus grace equals power. That's another one of God's paradoxes.

The words *bless, blessed,* and *blessing* are found over five hundred times in the Bible and describe such diverse things as rain, bumper crops, babies and, most important, salvation from sin. God blesses all kinds of people, among them Adam and Eve (Genesis 1:28; 5:2), Noah and his sons (Genesis 9:1), Ishmael (Genesis 17:20), and Samson (Judges 13:24). He blessed Abraham (Genesis 18:18), Sarah (Genesis 17:16), Isaac (Genesis 25:11), and Jacob (Genesis 35:9), and through them brought blessing to the whole world. Jacob brought God's blessing to his double-dealing father-in-law Laban (Genesis 30:27), and Joseph brought God's blessing to the household of Potiphar in Egypt (Genesis 39:5). These people—and many more—received God's blessings and shared them, and this enriched and enlarged their lives. At that time, events in their lives didn't seem like blessings, but they turned out to be the best things that ever happened to them.

So what is a blessing?

After surveying the biblical record, I have come to the conclusion that a blessing is any act of God that brings Him glory by accomplishing His will and helping His people grow and do His will. You can't buy blessings or manufacture them; they can come only from the Lord. You can't easily explain blessings—how they happen, when they happen, to whom they happen. When they occur, the best thing to do is to accept them and give thanks to God. God's blessings are gracious gifts from heaven that meet our needs in ways that build us up and help us glorify the Lord. "Bless the

Lord!" is the equivalent of "Praise the Lord!" and we ought to use those words more often.

It's worth noting that our English word *bless* is thought to come from the Old English verb *bletsian,* which meant, "to consecrate through blood." The Latin gives us *benediction* (to speak well of), and the Greek means "to eulogize." The major Hebrew word for *bless* is *barak,* the root of which means "to bow the knee in worship." God's blessing, then, involves a price to pay—the shed blood of Jesus—and a submission to the Lord that says, "Not my will, but your will be done." The shed blood and the bent knee.

There are *natural blessings* that the Lord sends to everybody, such as the air we breathe, the sunshine that helps things live and grow, the water we drink, and the food we eat. God blessed His creation (Genesis 1:22, 28; 5:2), and now His creation blesses us. God blessed the Sabbath day, and it became a blessing to Israel, until their religious leaders turned the blessing into a tedious burden (Matthew12:1–14; Mark 2:27).

Because of God's covenant with Israel, His people had a unique relationship to the natural blessings in creation. If they obeyed the Lord, He would send them regular rainfall and give them increased flocks and herds and bountiful harvests; but if they rebelled, those natural blessings would be removed (Leviticus 26; Deuteronomy 27–30). The arrangement was simple: obedience brought prosperity, and disobedience brought adversity. Whenever the Israelites turned away from God and started worshiping idols, God sent prophets to warn them of the terms of the covenant. If they persisted in disobeying, then He sent chastening to bring them to repentance. The book of Judges records at least seven such cycles.

We today who have trusted Jesus Christ and are under the new covenant cannot claim these old covenant blessings of health, wealth, and prosperity. But the principle of "faith and obedience bring blessing" still applies, even though the promised blessings may be different. The just still live by faith, and faith still leads to obedience, and obedience leads to God's blessing (Hebrews 10:38–39; James 2:14–26). We obey because we love Him, not because we want rewards; and that loving obedience of faith opens the way for the Lord to bless us and make us a blessing. Hebrews 11 proves that God has always honored the faith and obedience of those who trust and obey.

Considering who we are and what we do, it's remarkable that God wants to bless us at all, but He does. We are united to Christ by faith and share His life; therefore, the Father blesses us because of His Son. The Father is the source of "every good and perfect gift" (James 1:17), and our only access to Him is through Jesus Christ. We pray in the name of Jesus and for the glory of Jesus, and God's answers are His blessings to us.

But we must confess that we don't always recognize God's gifts as blessings. In fact, sometimes circumstances are so painful that we wonder if God really cares. Consider Jacob's limp, Joseph's exile and imprisonment in Egypt, David's conflicts with King Saul, Paul's thorn in the flesh, and especially the crucifixion of Jesus. At the time, these events looked like tragedies, but in God's time they became victories. Joseph had the right outlook when he said to his brothers, "You intended to harm me, but God intended it for good" (Genesis 50:20). That's the Old Testament version of Romans 8:28: "And we know that in all things God works for the good of those who love him, who have been called according to his purpose." And what is that purpose? That we might "be conformed to the likeness of his Son" (Romans 8:29).

The world complains about pain and difficult situations because the world lives primarily for happiness, but God's people learn to rejoice in their sufferings (Romans 5:1–5) because our goal is *holiness*, growing to be more like Jesus Christ—and that is our happiness. "Blessed are those who hunger and thirst for righteousness, for they will be filled" (Matthew 5:6). Who can mind the process when the end product is likeness to Christ?

Scattered throughout the Bible, but especially in the New Testament epistles, are statements that we call *benedictions*. The English word means "to speak well; to speak something good." For centuries, Christian worship services ended with the leader pronouncing a scriptural benediction upon the gathered believers before they departed. For some reason—maybe to make us more "seeker friendly"—many services today don't end with this added blessing. Instead, the worship leader or speaker says, "Well, thanks for being here. You are dismissed." Or the leader might promote some future meeting and then let the people go home. I prefer a benediction to a folksy goodbye. If pronouncing a benediction was a blessing throughout twenty centuries of church history, why abandon it now?

In these pages, we will examine the most prominent benedictions in the Bible and seek to learn what the blessings are that God wants us to receive from Him and share with others. We are blessed that we might be a blessing; we are channels of God's blessing, not reservoirs. Yes, it's a blessing to receive—and I want this book to be a blessing to you— but Jesus said, "It is more blessed to give than to receive" (Acts 20:35). He also said, "Give, and it will be given to you" (Luke 6:38).

Learning from the Bible will not automatically bring us God's blessings. We are blessed in *doing* the Word and not just in reading or studying it (James 1:22–25). If we determine that we want to *be* a blessing and not just *get* blessing, then the Lord will help us translate learning into living, and blessings will be ours to share. He has already blessed us with "every spiritual blessing in Christ" (Ephesians 1:3), and by faith we may draw from that treasury. The Lord will say to us as He said to Abraham, "I will bless you . . . and you will be a blessing" (Genesis 12:2).

I invite you to become a "benediction believer."

CHAPTER 2

THE BENEDICTION OF ISRAEL

The Lord said to Moses, "Tell Aaron and his sons, 'This is how you are to bless the Israelites. Say to them: "The Lord bless you and keep you; the Lord make his face shine upon you and be gracious to you; the Lord turn his face toward you and give you peace."' So they will put my name on the Israelites, and I will bless them" (Numbers 6:22–27).

THIS BENEDICTION MAY BE the most quoted of all the benedictions. Not only do Christian ministers pronounce this benediction as they conclude church worship services, but Jewish rabbis also use it to close synagogue services. The New Testament parallel would be the Trinitarian benediction in 2 Corinthians 13:14: "May the grace of the Lord Jesus Christ, and the love of God, and the fellowship of the Holy Spirit be with you all."

Twice the Lord told Moses that this benediction was especially for "the Israelites," the descendants of Jacob, who was also called Israel. God commanded that the priests be the custodians of these words because they alone were allowed to speak them in the public assemblies. The priests were privileged to serve God and His people by teaching and applying the law, offering sacrifices, and praying and publicly blessing the congregation. Even today, any acceptable man in the synagogue family is permitted to pray publicly, but only a rabbi may pronounce this or any other benediction.

On the day the priests were ordained and the tabernacle was dedicated, Aaron and Moses offered the sacrifices God command-ed, went into the tabernacle, and then came out for Aaron to lift his hands and bless the people. This was undoubtedly the blessing he used. It was then that God's glory appeared and fire from heaven consumed the burnt offering on the altar. The people shouted for joy as they fell on their faces in awe before the Lord (Leviticus 9:23–24). During the years of the second temple, each morning, between the offering of the incense and the sacrifice of the burnt offering, five priests stood on the temple steps and pronounced this benediction. This reminds us that it is the sacrifice of Jesus on the cross that makes possible the spiritual blessings God has poured out on His people. We want to consider three aspects of this benediction, for it is the benediction of Israel the nation; Israel the man, who founded the twelve tribes of Israel; and "the Israel of God" that Paul mentions in Galatians 6:16.

ISRAEL THE NATION
Provision and Protection

The six "you" pronouns in this benediction are all singular, indicating that God's blessing was for the individual. He is the God of Abraham and of Isaac and of Jacob, the God of individual believers. But twice the Lord mentions the Israelites, so the entire nation is promised a blessing. Israel is the only nation in history that has entered into a covenant relationship with the Lord (Psalm 147:20). It began when God called Abraham and said, "I will make you into a great nation and I will bless you; I will make your name great, and you will be a blessing. I will bless those who bless you, and whoever curses you I will curse; and all peoples on earth will be blessed through you" (Genesis 12:2–3).

The apostle Paul tells us some of the blessings the Lord gave to the Jewish nation: "Theirs is the adoption as sons; theirs the divine glory, the covenants, the receiving of the law, the temple worship and the promises. Theirs are the patriarchs, and from them is traced the human ancestry of Christ, who is God over all, forever praised! Amen" (Romans 9:3–5).

What a treasury of blessings! In His sovereign grace, God chose Jews to be His special people, not because they were numerous or powerful, but because He loved them and kept the unchanging promise He made to their forefathers (Deuteronomy 7:7–9). He gave them His law, promising to bless them if they obeyed and to chasten them if they rebelled. He gave them the tabernacle and the temple, and His glory dwelt in both. Other nations had temples, but they were empty. Perhaps the greatest blessing of all was the privilege of bringing the Savior and Messiah into the world. I have received from the Jews the greatest treasures I possess: the knowledge of the true and living God; the Holy Scriptures; and the Lord Jesus Christ, my Savior. Indeed, Israel has been a blessing to the whole world.

The Lord also gave His people a land in which to live, and as long as they obeyed God's law, He would care for the land and bless their labors (Deuteronomy 11:8–32). Alas, the people frequently rebelled against the Lord, and He punished them in their land. (See the book of Judges for an account of Israel's disobedience and chastisement.) They persisted in their disobedience, so He finally took them out of the land and chastened them in Babylon for seventy years. Broken and bankrupt, they returned to their land, only to be in bondage to one Gentile empire after another—Media-Persia, Greece, Egypt, Syria, and Rome. After Rome's destruction of Jerusalem in AD 70, the nation was scattered.

Though they were dispersed around the world, the Jewish people were never assimilated into the other nations, and no nation has succeeded in destroying Israel. From pharaoh in Egypt to the latest dictator, every nation that tried to exterminate the Jewish people was itself defeated. God has watched over His chosen people throughout the centuries, and they are still with us. The Lord blessed them, and the Lord has kept them and will continue to keep them.

Glory and Grace

Unlike the pagan idols Israel's neighbors worshiped, Jehovah God is spirit and therefore doesn't have a human body (see Psalm 115); but the Bible uses our human physical characteristics to help describe how God relates to us and works for us. He has no eyes or ears, yet He sees us and hears us when we pray (Psalm 34:15). He has no feet, yet He walks with us (Genesis 5:22–24); He has no mouth yet speaks to us (Isaiah 1:20; 40:5). God's face shining upon Israel meant that He was pleased and delighted with them, and therefore He blessed them. Nobody deserves the blessing of God. His smiling face and generous heart are because of His grace, and not our merit.

Many people ask God's blessing before they partake of a meal, but the Jews were instructed also to give thanks after the meal was eaten. "When you have eaten and are satisfied, praise the Lord your God for the good land he has given you" (Deuteronomy 8:10). Why? The answer is in Deuteronomy 6:11–12: "Then when you eat and are satisfied, be careful that you do not forget the Lord." When our blessings are more meaningful to us than the God who gave them, we've taken the first step toward idolatry. It delights the heart of God when His children are thankful for the Giver, and not just the gifts.

But God's shining face reminds us also of the sun. "For the Lord God is a sun and shield; the Lord bestows favor and honor; no good thing does he withhold from those whose walk is blameless" (Psalm 84:11). "But for you who revere my name, the son of righteousness will rise with healing in its wings" (Malachi 4:2). Zechariah, the father of John the Baptist, described the birth of Jesus as the dawning of a new day for those in darkness (Luke 1:78–79), and Jesus Himself claimed to be "the light of the world" (John 8:12). Just as the sun is the source of light and life for this earth, so Jesus is the giver of light and life to His people. "In him was life, and that life was the light of men" (John 1:4). If God sent each inhabitant of the earth a bill for one year's sunlight, we would all be bankrupt. It is pure grace that "He causes his sun to rise on the evil and the good, and sends rain on the righteous and the unrighteous" (Matthew 5:45). Israel has glory and grace as well as provision and protection.

Reconciliation and Rest

If God's people Israel have received these blessings from the Lord, why have they suffered so much, and why don't they trust Jesus as their Messiah? Reviewing three murders in the history of Israel will help to answer that question.

God promised to send a messenger to prepare Israel for the coming of His Son and their Messiah, and that messenger was John the Baptist (Mark 1:1–8; Malachi 3:1; Isaiah 40:1–3). Because John rebuked Herod Antipas for taking his brother Philip's wife, Herod had John arrested and put into prison and eventually killed him (Matthew 14:1–12). As far as the record is concerned, not one Jewish leader interceded for John to try to secure his release. The nation simply allowed John to be killed and sinned against God the Father who sent him.

Jesus, the Son of God, came and ministered to the nation and proved that He was indeed their promised Messiah, but the leaders rejected Him and persuaded the people to ask Pilate to crucify Him. The leaders allowed John the Baptist to be slain and then asked for Jesus to be slain. In doing this, they sinned against God the Son.

Jesus arose from the dead, ascended to heaven, and sent the Holy Spirit to live in His people and empower them for witness. Stephen the deacon was filled with the Spirit, and his witness for Jesus confounded the unbelieving Jews, who had him arrested (Acts 6:8–15). The nation of Israel had allowed John the Baptist to be killed and had sinned against the Father; they had asked for Jesus to be killed and sinned against the Son; *and now they themselves killed Stephen and sinned against the Holy Spirit!* "You stiff-necked people," said Stephen. "You always resist the Holy Spirit!" (Acts 7:51). This was the sin against the Spirit that Jesus had warned about in Matthew 12:30–32, a sin for which there is no forgiveness.

Israel, in the name of religion, having rejected Jehovah God—the Father, the Son, and the Spirit—would now experience the hiding of God's face from them and the pain of conflict and judgment. God told Moses that his people would forsake the Lord and break His covenant. "On that day I will become angry with them and forsake them; I will hide my face from them, and they will be destroyed" (Deuteronomy 31:17; see Isaiah 66). For the Lord, to "hide His face" meant temporary rejection of Israel and loss of blessing, and that is the spiritual condition of Israel today. God has not withdrawn His love nor revoked His covenant (Romans 11:28–32), but because of Israel's fall, the gospel has gone to the Gentiles.

There is a coming day when God will turn his face toward His people Israel and give them peace. They have suffered as no other nation, but they will one day see their Messiah, repent of their sins, and trust in Him and be saved. "They will look on me, the one they have pierced," promises the Lord, and "[on] that day a fountain will be opened to the house of David and the inhabitants of Jerusalem, to cleanse them from sin and iniquity" (Zechariah 12:10, 13:1).

"Pray for the peace of Jerusalem" (Psalm 122:6), for there can be no peace in this world until the Prince of Peace (Isaiah 9:6) reigns in the city of peace.

ISRAEL THE MAN (JACOB)

THREE OUTSTANDING EXPERIENCES with the Lord transformed Jacob into a man of God and a channel of God's blessing to others.

Bethel: God's Blessing and Promise (Genesis 28:10–21)

Here we meet Jacob, the fugitive son, fleeing from his angry brother Esau. He was heading for the home of his Uncle Laban in Padan

Aram, where he hoped to stay long enough to marry a wife, establish a family, and give his brother time to cool off. Until that day, life had been fairly easy for Jacob, but now he was at a hard place in the road and didn't know what to do. But God in His grace met Jacob in a dream, spoke to him, and sent him on his way with divine assurances to encourage him. Jacob had lived a life based on human wisdom and clever schemes, but from now on he had to live by faith in the promises of God.

God assured Jacob that *He would bless him* (Genesis 28:10–14). This included giving him the land of Canaan and descendants that would multiply greatly and be like the dust of the earth. Even more, Jacob's descendants would be a blessing to the whole world, just as God promised Abraham (Genesis 12:1–3).

The Lord also promised Jacob that *He would be with him and keep him safe* (Genesis 28:15). What a promise: "I will not leave you until I have done what I have promised you." This is the Old Testament version of Hebrews 13:5 and Philippians 1:6. Jacob's father-in-law Laban lied to him and cheated him, but the Lord was with Jacob and protected him and blessed him. Jacob started his pilgrimage asking, "How can I get out of this?" but soon learned that the real question was, "*What* can I get out of this?"

Peniel: God's Shining Face (Genesis 32:22–32)

Jacob, the fugitive son, was now Jacob, the frightened brother. He had been with Laban for twenty years, and the time had come for him to take his family, flocks, and herds and return home. God's blessing had made Jacob a wealthy man, and though Laban tried to stop him, the Lord kept His promise and protected Jacob and enabled him to confront his father-in-law unafraid. God had promised to bring him back to his land (Genesis 28:15), and He kept His promise.

But before Jacob met Isaac, he had to meet his brother Esau, who was coming to him with four hundred men. We can't run away from the past, and Jacob was certain that Esau was bent on revenge. Jacob wasn't at all prepared for a battle, so he once again resorted to his scheming. First, he sent expensive gifts to his brother, hoping to pacify him. Then he divided his family and put them into safe places, and now he was left alone to wrestle with God.

Jacob fought with the Lord all that night, but he found his victory in submitting and not struggling. Jacob was too "wise" and too "strong" for God to use him, so God weakened him, for when we are weak only then are we strong (2 Corinthians 12:7–10). Jacob saw the face of God (*Peniel* means "face of God") and knew he was forgiven and accepted. The victorious Christian life is a series of new beginnings, and this was a new start for Jacob. He had a new experience of the grace of God and was given a new name—Israel—which is variously translated as "prince with God," "a God-conquered man," or "he struggles with God."

God could have scolded Jacob for some of the things he had done, but there was no word of reproof. Instead, God's face had shined upon him, and God had been gracious to him and his family. "Restore us, O God; make your face shine upon us, that we may be saved" (Psalm 80:3, 7, 19).

Egypt: God's Smile and Peace (Genesis 46:1–4; 47–49)

Jacob is now the faithful pilgrim. For years he had been saying, "Everything is against me!" (Genesis 42:36), but now he would learn that everything had been working for him (Romans 8:28). Joseph was alive, and God had prepared a refuge in Egypt for Jacob. But before Jacob went to Egypt, he paused to worship God, and the Lord assured him that it was His will that he go. Abraham had gone to Egypt and gotten into trouble, but that wouldn't happen to Jacob. He would go to Egypt and be a blessing. God had smiled upon him and given him peace.

It was a time for peace, and that comes from righteousness. "The fruit of righteousness will be peace; the effect of righteousness will be quietness and confidence forever" (Isaiah 32:17). God had frowned on Jacob's sons for hating their brother Joseph, selling him as a slave, and deceiving their father into thinking he was dead. But now God's face was shining, and it was time for peace. Joseph's patient dealing with his brothers had brought them to the place of confession, and he and his brothers were reconciled. Jacob no doubt realized the mistake he had made in preferring Joseph, but all of that was now history. Did the brothers apologize to their father for causing him grief for so many years? We hope so.

Jacob had brought blessing to Laban, and he also brought blessing to Egypt. He blessed Pharaoh, who was at that time the most powerful ruler in the ancient Near East. He blessed Joseph and his two sons, and before he died, Jacob blessed all of his sons and prophesied what would befall them. Reuben, Jacob's firstborn by Leah, lost the blessing of the firstborn because of his sin, and the blessing was given to Joseph, Jacob's firstborn by Rachel. Led by the Lord, Jacob prepared the men who founded the twelve tribes of Israel. The tribes would remain in Egypt for many years and then would go forth a mighty nation. What a spiritual giant Jacob had become!

"God . . . has been my shepherd," Jacob told Joseph and his two sons (Genesis 48:15), and he repeated the shepherd image in Genesis 49:24. The Jewish people confessed that they were Jehovah's flock and "the sheep of his pasture" (Psalm 100:3). Believers today have Jesus as their Good Shepherd (John 10:1–18), Great Shepherd (Hebrews 13:20–21), and Chief Shepherd (1 Peter 5:4), and He will be our Shepherd for all eternity (Revelation 7:17).

The fugitive son became the fearful brother, but the fearful brother became the faithful pilgrim—and he was a pilgrim to the end. "By faith Jacob, when he was dying, blessed each of Joseph's sons, and worshiped as he leaned on the top of his staff" (Hebrews 11:21). In life, he needed that pilgrim staff because he had a limp; now in death, he reminded his sons that life is a blessing and ends in peace only when you are a pilgrim and walk by faith in the Lord.

After a difficult life, Jacob the pilgrim died in peace, and God was smiling upon him as He welcomed him to glory.

THE ISRAEL OF GOD (GALATIANS 6:16)

PAUL'S LETTER TO the Galatian churches deals primarily with the relationship of the Jewish law to the message of grace. As recorded in Acts 15, false teachers had told the Gentile converts that they had to obey the law of Moses in order to be saved and grow in their spiritual walk. Paul pointed out that all true believers are the "spiritual children of Abraham" and share in God's promised blessing (Galatians 3:6–15). In Jesus Christ, there is neither Jew nor Gentile; we are all a new creation in Christ and members of His body. "If you belong to Christ, then you are Abraham's seed, and heirs according to the promise" (Galatians 3:28–29).

All believers have experienced the spiritual circumcision (Philippians 3:2–3) and are not required to live by the old covenant law. The church came out of Israel and shares in the spiritual blessings of Abraham, but the church is not Israel. There is continuity but not identity. What Israel was to the Lord under the old covenant, the church is to Him under the new covenant. "But you are a chosen people, a royal priesthood, a holy nation, a people belonging to God" (1 Peter 2:9; see Exodus 19:1–6). Jesus said to the leaders of Israel, "Therefore I tell you that the kingdom of God will be taken away from you and given to a people who will produce its fruit" (Matthew 21:43).

God Blesses the Church and Keeps It

The church can say with Israel, "The Lord is my shepherd, I shall not be in want" and "I will fear no evil" (Psalm 23:1, 4). Because Jesus is our Shepherd, as we trust and follow Him, we always have provision and protection.

Consider these three verses.

Praise be to the God and Father of our Lord Jesus Christ, who has blessed us in the heavenly realms with every spiritual blessing in Christ (Ephesians 1:3).

Praise be to the God and Father of our Lord Jesus Christ, . . . who comforts us in all our troubles . . . (2 Corinthians 1:3–4).

Praise be to the God and Father of our Lord Jesus Christ! In his great mercy he has given us new birth into a living hope through the resurrection of Jesus Christ from the dead, and into an inheritance that can never perish, spoil or fade . . . (1 Peter 1:3–4).

In the first verse, Paul looks *back* and praises the Father for all the blessings that have already been given to His people in Christ. We have every spiritual blessing and lack nothing that we need in the spiritual realm. In the second verse, Paul praises the Father that *today* we have all the comfort and encouragement that we need because He is "the God of all comfort." The third verse is from Peter and praises the Father for the *future* blessings that we have in Christ, the "living hope," and the eternal inheritance that can never fade away.

What a wealthy people we are in Jesus Christ! We can by faith claim "every spiritual blessing" and all the comfort and encouragement we need, and we can look forward to enjoying an eternal inheritance with Him. These three inspired statements lay down no conditions because they are guaranteed in Christ. The Old Testament Jew had definite covenant conditions he had to meet before he could receive God's blessings. New covenant believers already have the blessings and need only claim them by faith. "Since, then, you have been raised with Christ, set your hearts on things above, where Christ is seated at the right hand of God" (Colossians 3:1).

The Lord not only blesses His church, but also He keeps His church. "My sheep listen to my voice; I know them, and they follow me. I give them eternal life, and they shall never perish; no one can snatch them out of my hand. My Father, who has given them to me, is greater than all; no one can snatch them out of my Father's hand" (John 10:27–29). Jesus didn't say that He protected everybody who claimed to be a Christian, but only those who proved they are His because they listen to His voice and follow Him. "Not everyone who says to me, 'Lord, Lord,' will enter the kingdom of heaven, but only he who does the will of my Father who is in heaven" (Matthew 7:21).

Jesus prayed that His true disciples would be with Him in heaven, and the Father always answers the prayers of His Son (John 11:41–42). "Father, I want those you have given me to be with me where I am, and to see my glory, the glory you have given me because you loved me before the creation of the world" (John 17:24). When a believer dies, the Father answers this prayer and takes that soul to heaven to dwell in the place Jesus has prepared (John 14:1–6).

He blesses us and keeps us! What a wonderful Savior we have!

God Makes His Face to Shine on Us and Is Gracious to Us

The Old Testament believer wrote, "For the Lord God is a sun and shield" (Psalm 84:11), and Jesus said to His disciples, "I am the light of the world" (John 8:12). Christians are the "children of light" (Ephesians 5:8) and therefore should "walk in the light" (1 John 1:7). What the sun is to our universe, Jesus is to His people—the source of light and life. If we want to know where we are going, we must live in the light. If we want to produce fruit for His glory, we must live in the light, "for the fruit of the light consists in all goodness, righteousness and truth" (Ephesians 5:9).

When the Father looks upon His children and smiles with pleasure, then His grace begins to work in our lives. To us, He is "the God of all grace" (1 Peter 5:10), and His glorious throne is a "throne of grace." We come to Him and ask our needs to be met, and we "receive mercy and find grace to help us in our time of need" (Hebrews 4:16).

Because we belong to Jesus Christ, God in His mercy doesn't give us what we do deserve—judgment—but in His grace He gives us what we don't deserve. If we pray on the basis of our character or conduct and hint that we have earned His blessings, then we are not praying at a throne of grace. We are practicing some form of subtle legalism. This doesn't mean we can live any way we please and expect to have our prayers answered, because abiding in Christ is a condition for answered prayer (John 15:7). The closer we get to the light, the more we see how soiled we are, and the less we feel that we deserve anything from the Lord. We entered God's family by grace (Ephesians 2:8–9), and it's only by grace that we can enjoy the family. I will have more to say about this when we study the benediction of the Trinity in the next chapter.

We must never forget that God is gracious. Moses learned this on Mount Sinai when he interceded for sinful Israel. He heard God say, "The Lord, the Lord, the compassionate and gracious God . . ." (Exodus 34:6). King Hezekiah reminded the people of Judah that God was gracious and compassionate (2 Chronicles 30:9), and so did Ezra (9:8) and Nehemiah (9:17, 31). Paul made God's gracious dealings a cornerstone of his theology: "He who did not spare his own Son, but gave him up for us all—how will he not also, along with him, graciously give us all things?"(Romans 8:32). If God graciously gave us Jesus, the best that He had, what would keep Him from giving us the lesser gifts that we need? "Yet the Lord longs to be gracious to you; he rises to show you compassion" (Isaiah 30:18).

God Lifts His Countenance to Us and Gives Us Peace

As we have seen, the image of God's countenance turned toward us refers to His turning back to bless His people after they have disobeyed Him and asked for His forgiveness. Israel frequently asked, "Why do you hide your face and forget our misery and oppression?" (Psalm 44:24). If the Lord hides His face, it's because we have offended and grieved Him. Our responsibility is to repent, confess our sins, and seek His face. "Let the light of your face shine upon us, O Lord" (Psalm 4:6).

The church today needs the smile of God's face. The church needs to repent and turn from its worldly ways and seek the face of the Lord when it sins, yet how few churches have prayer meetings and pray for revival. I recall hearing Vance Havner say, "The last words of Jesus to the church are not the Great Commission in Matthew 28:18–20. His last words are 'Repent or else!' You will find them in the letters to the seven churches in Revelation chapters two and three." The church calls lost sinners to repent, and rightly so, but God also calls His church to repent. The Lord said to King Solomon: "If my people, who are called by my name, will humble themselves and pray and seek my face and turn from their wicked ways, then will I hear from heaven and will forgive their sin and will heal their land (2 Chronicles 7:14).

God's smile is the secret of peace in the heart of the individual believer and in the church congregation. How many churches have experienced quarrels and splits and refused to humble themselves before God to seek His face—yet they expect to enjoy His blessings. In recent years, some churches have called "solemn assemblies" for the purpose of confessing sin and seeking the face of God.

Churches and denominations boast about their budgets, their membership statistics, and their building programs, but none of these is a guarantee that the Lord is smiling upon them. Liberal churches and false cults have buildings, budgets, and crowds. The next time you come home from church with a smug satisfaction of success in your heart, sit down and carefully read the first chapter of Isaiah as God's message to us today and not just to ancient Israel.

The Hebrew word *shalom* that is translated "peace" is a rich word indeed. It means much more than "the absence of war." It includes health and happiness, satisfaction and completion, kindness, agreement, salvation, friendship, and the richness of a full life. With this in mind, read Isaiah 1 again and see if Judah was experiencing those gifts from God. Is the church today experiencing them?

It is possible for "the Israel of God" to be guilty of the same sins as the Israel of Scripture? When that happens, it is time for the church to humble itself and pray and seek God's face as it turns from its wicked ways.

CHAPTER 3

THE BENEDICTION OF THE TRINITY

May the grace of the Lord Jesus Christ, and the love of God, and the fellowship of the Holy Spirit be with you all (2 Corinthians 13:14).

I T'S MONDAY, JULY 16, 1945. It's 5:30 in the morning.
A blinding flash suddenly awakens the sleepy village of Carrizozo, New Mexico. Two minutes later there is a deafening roar. The first atomic bomb has been detonated thirty-five miles away, and a new age has been ushered in.

Less than a month later, on August 6, President Harry Truman announced to the nation that an atomic bomb had been dropped on the Japanese city of Hiroshima. He said, "We have spent two billion dollars on the greatest scientific gamble in history—and won." Hiroshima was almost completely destroyed, and seventy thousand people died instantly. In the weeks following, thousands more perished.

Oddly enough, the code name for the atomic bomb project was Trinity.

———

"CODE NAME TRINITY."

Would most people equate the Christian doctrine of the Trinity with the power and excitement of an atomic blast? Probably not. Many Christians deliberately avoid the doctrine. "We can't understand it," they argue, "and what difference does it make in our lives anyway?" Even Thomas Jefferson wrote, "Ideas must be distinct before reason can act upon them, and no man has a distinct idea of the Trinity. It is the mere Abracadabra of the mountebanks calling themselves the priests of Jesus."[1]

Some people say, "The word *trinity* isn't even found in the Bible, so why make an issue of it?" But if the silence of the Bible is evidence of non-existence, then we are really in trouble, for there are many words not found in Scripture that describe things that certainly exist.

Our benediction is a trinity of trinities. When we understand what Paul wrote, it will help us better relate to the Lord we worship and live a better Christian life in this world.

A TRINITY OF PERSONS

THE BIBLE REVEALS that there is one eternal God, with one essence, existing in three persons who are equal yet distinct: God the Father and God the Son and God the Holy Spirit. Note that in the preceding sentence I used the word *and,* and not a series of commas. The Father and the Son and the Holy Spirit are not sequential, like the ranks in an army—the Father first, the Spirit last, and Jesus between them—because each one is eternal God, and no one member of the Godhead is greater than another. In the baptismal formula (Matthew 28:19), Jesus named the Father first, then the Son, and then the Spirit, and He united them with the word *and.* In this benediction, Paul put the Son first, but that doesn't mean He is greater or more important than the Father and the Holy Spirit, because the little word *and* is still there to connect equals.

These are not three gods or different names for one God who reveals Himself in different ways at different times. The heretics say, "The one God revealed Himself as the Father in the Old Testament, as the Son in the four gospels, and as the Spirit from the Pentecost to the end of the New Testament." Anyone who believes that hasn't read the Bible carefully.

The Trinity worked together in the creation of the universe (Genesis 1:1–2; Job 38:4; Psalm 104:30; Colossians 1:16–17). While the fullness of this doctrine wasn't revealed until centuries later, the persons of the Godhead were there from the beginning. They had been there from eternity.

Listen to the angel Gabriel explain to Mary how the miracle of the incarnation would occur: "The Holy Spirit will come upon you, and the power of the Most High will overshadow you. So the holy one to be born will be called the Son of God" (Luke 1:35). Each member of the Godhead would play a part—the Spirit, the Father, and the Son. If the Father belonged in the Old Testament and the Spirit in the Acts and epistles, this miracle could never have happened.

Or visit the Jordan River as John the Baptist is baptizing Jesus of Nazareth: "As soon as Jesus was baptized, he went up out of the water. At that moment heaven was opened, and he saw the Spirit of God descending like a dove and lighting on him. And a voice from heaven said, 'This is my Son, whom I love; with him I am well pleased'" (Matthew 3:16–17). Once again, the Trinity is working together: the Son obeys, the Spirit descends, and the Father speaks.

When Jesus began His public ministry at Nazareth, the first words He spoke were from the prophet Isaiah (61:1–2): "The Spirit of the Sovereign Lord is on me . . ." Here is the Trinity: the Spirit and the Father (Lord) and the Son. Peter picked up this theme when he gave his message in the home of the Roman centurion Cornelius: "how God anointed Jesus of Nazareth with the Holy Spirit and power" (Acts 10:38). We see the Trinity again as Peter explains the functions of the Father and the Son and the Holy Spirit.

When Jesus taught His disciples in the upper room (John 13–16), His doctrine was Trinitarian. "And I will ask the Father, and he will give you another Counselor to be with you forever—the

Spirit of truth" (John 14:16). "But the Counselor, the Holy Spirit, whom the Father will send in my name, will teach you all things" (John 14:26). "When the Counselor comes, whom I will send to you from the Father, the Spirit of truth" (John 15:26). There's no confusion of persons here.

In Jesus' death on the cross, all the persons of the Godhead were involved. "How much more, then, will the blood of Christ, who through the eternal Spirit offered himself unblemished to God, cleanse our consciences!" (Hebrews 9:14). Peter announced at Pentecost that the Godhead was also involved in Christ's resurrection: "God has raised this Jesus to life, and we are all witnesses of the fact. Exalted to the right hand of God, he has received from the Father the promised Holy Spirit and has poured out what you now see and hear" (Acts 2:32–33).

Every sinner who has ever trusted Jesus Christ has experienced the saving work of the Trinity. Paul's hymn in Ephesians 1:3–14 extols the triune God: the Father for electing us (vv. 3–6), the Son for dying for us (vv. 7–12), and the Spirit for sealing us (vv. 13–14). Paul condenses the truth of this hymn in Titus 3:4–6, Galatians 4:4–6, and 2 Corinthians 1:21–22. Peter condenses the salvation work of the Trinity into one verse: "God's elect . . . chosen according to the foreknowledge of God the Father, through the sanctifying work of the Spirit, for obedience to Jesus Christ and sprinkling by his blood" (1 Peter 1:1–2).

The skeptics and scoffers try to use mathematics to refute the truth of the Trinity: "One god + one god + one god = three gods." But the persons of the Godhead exist in a dynamic relationship, so the correct "formula" is $1 \times 1 \times 1 = 1$. "No fact more directly establishes the uniqueness of the Christian view of God than that of the Trinity," wrote Dr. Carl F. H. Henry.[2] Orthodox Jews and Moslems believe in one God, as do orthodox Christians, but orthodox Jews and Moslems do not believe in the deity of Jesus the Son or the personality and deity of the Holy Spirit. They are not Trinitarian.

Obviously, there is much in the doctrine of the Trinity that is beyond human comprehension and explanation. In his magnificent treatise *On the Trinity*, Augustine wrote, "God is greater and truer in our thoughts than in our words; he is greater and truer in reality than in our thoughts." In spite of what Thomas Jefferson believed, there are truths known in the heart that cannot easily be defined in the mind or expressed by the lips. Theology often ends in silence and worship.

Christians worship the Triune God. Any other kind of worship is not Christian. The late Dr. James S. Stewart of Edinburgh wrote, "What [the critics] are needing most is to stop discussing and get down on their knees. That is the only attitude in which the ultimate truths of religion are ever discerned."[3]

A Trinity of Privileges

Nowhere in the Bible is there a book or a section of a book devoted to explaining the doctrine of the Trinity. Just as the truth of the deity of Jesus gradually dawned upon His disciples, climaxing in Peter's declaration of faith (Matthew 16:16), so the truth of the Trinity grew out of the personal spiritual experiences of the first Christians. As daily they worshiped the God of Abraham, Isaac, and Jacob; walked with Jesus; and depended on the Spirit, this marvelous truth took hold of them. James S. Stewart explains, "It began when men made this discovery—that they could not say all they meant by the word 'God' until they had said Father, Son and Spirit."[4] Once this truth gripped the disciples, Scriptures took on new meaning, their ministry took on new power, and their personal Christian walk new depth.

Christian historians point out that the church itself had to recover these truths in order to experience renewal and revival. The Reformation recovered the truth of God's grace in justification by faith, not by merit or good works. When academics almost froze the heart of the church, various pietistic movements restored the importance of loving God personally and enjoying His presence intimately. In recent years, the ministry of the Holy Spirit has been foremost, and we've learned to depend on His wisdom and power. The life of the Christian must be Trinitarian, or we will be living beneath our spiritual privileges. Now, let's consider some of them.

The Grace of the Lord Jesus Christ

The early believers knew that their salvation was wholly by grace, for there was no other way to be saved. But they also learned that they had to *live* by grace, for without Jesus, they could do nothing (John 15:5). As the four Gospels and the apostolic letters circulated among the churches, the believers discovered the riches of God's grace; as they served and suffered, they experienced that grace personally. The Scriptures were "the word of his grace" (Acts 20:32). And the Spirit of grace (Hebrews 10:29) taught them divine truth and enabled them to obey it.

In the early years of the expansion of the church, there were theological conflicts over law and grace, and some of those conflicts are still with us. The legalistic Jewish believers emphasized obeying the demands of the law, while the Gentile believers rejoiced in the freedom of obedience in the grace of Christ. The law of Moses is a heavy yoke to bear (Acts 15:10), but the yoke of Christ is "easy" and "light" (Matthew 11:28–30). That's grace! The law was a guardian or "babysitter," but God's grace treats us like mature children who can draw upon their rich inheritance (Galatians 4:1–7). The precepts of the law were mere shadows, but by grace we have the living reality in Christ (Colossians 2:16–17). The law is a mirror that reveals the sinner's defilement (James 1:22–25), but the mirror cannot wash it away. Christians today look into the mirror of the Word, a glorious mirror that reveals the face of Jesus Christ and transforms us into His glory (2 Corinthians 3:7–18). Law condemns—grace transforms!

There's nothing sinful about establishing standards and setting goals; but the minute we try to meet the standards and attain the goals *in our own strength*, we have moved from grace to law, and we will fail. Paul's testimony should also be our testimony: "But by the grace of God I am what I am, and his grace to me was not without effect" (1 Corinthians 15:10). The life controlled by grace brings great glory to the Lord because nobody can explain it.

Simply because grace is free doesn't mean that grace is cheap. Grace is costly. "For you know the grace of our Lord Jesus Christ, that though he was rich, yet for your sakes he became poor, so that you through his poverty might become rich" (2 Corinthians 8:9). The only way we can be rich in grace is to be poor in ourselves and to trust in God to help us. It costs us nothing to add the word *grace* to our theological vocabulary, but it costs us dearly to practice grace in everyday life. It cost Jesus everything to bring God's grace to us, and it should cost us to bring that grace to others. "Cheap grace is the deadly enemy of our church," wrote the martyred theologian Dietrich Bonhoeffer. "Cheap grace is grace without discipleship."[5]

The Love of God

It's difficult to maintain a life of love because we live in a world that's heavily controlled by competition and greatly polluted by violent words and deeds. We have no problem loving those who love us, but to love those who hate us and hate our Jesus Christ is quite another matter. We think that the easiest way to live is to avoid our enemies and enjoy our Christian brothers and sisters, but Jesus tells us that even the tax collectors and pagans can do that. He expects us to love our enemies, pray for them, and do good to them (Matthew 5:43–48). In this way we imitate the Father, who daily gives free sunshine to all kinds of people all over the world and then adds the rain with it. Most people take these loving gifts for granted and don't even say thanks. If the Lord sent us an annual bill for these blessings, we would go broke trying to pay it.

When you and I were born into this world, we were selfish and demanding, because, as infants, crying was the only way we could communicate our discomfort and needs. We had to let everybody know when we were hungry, uncomfortable, bored, and tired, and our caregivers came to our rescue. But as we grew up, our parents and siblings let us know that such childish behavior was unacceptable. We had to learn to feed ourselves, to walk, to speak, to dress ourselves, to pick up our toys, and to keep ourselves out of trouble. Whenever we lapsed into childish attitudes and actions, we were warned and perhaps disciplined and told to grow up.

When our lives are motivated more and more by the love of God, it's evidence that we're maturing spiritually. "God has poured out his love into our hearts by the Holy Spirit, whom he has given us" (Romans 5:5), and that love changes our attitudes and actions. The fruit of the Spirit is love (Galatians 5:22). We don't manufacture love. We yield to the Holy Spirit, obey God's Word by faith, and let the Spirit work in and through us. Often the Lord brings unlovable people into our lives, perhaps people who even profess to be Christians, and we have to get along with them. But this is one of the Lord's ways of cultivating His love in our hearts. It's hard to love people who make life difficult for us, but these people can help us grow in grace and become stronger in faith and love.

Christian love isn't a temporary shallow "fuzzy feeling" towards people; it's a determined and sacrificial act of the will. Love doesn't just feel; it goes to work. "For God so loved the world that he gave his one and only Son" (John 3:16). "Greater love has no one than this, that he lay down his life for his friends" (John 15:13). Jesus didn't just feel sorry for us; He did what was necessary to save us.

Depending on "religious feelings" can lead us astray. As we leave the worship service, we love everybody, and then we discover that somebody has sculptured the front fender of our car in the parking lot. As I took my seat on a commuter plane, I smiled at the young father sitting behind me with two children. As the plane took off, one of the children began to scream, and the other one threw up. I didn't feel like smiling, but I knew I'd better let God's love take over.

God is our loving Father, and the world we live in is our Father's world. He is in control, but He doesn't necessarily arrange things to keep us comfortable or to make life easier. Sometimes He permits just the opposite to occur, and we find ourselves nervous and upset and looking for somebody to blame instead of somebody to love. We start groaning instead of growing, and another opportunity is lost for glorifying the Father.

"As the Father has loved me," said Jesus to His disciples, "so have I loved you. Now remain in my love . . . If anyone loves me, he will obey my teaching. My Father will love him, and we will come to him and make our home with him" (John 15:9; 14:23). Keep yourselves in God's love," admonishes Jude 21. This doesn't mean that we must work hard to merit God's love, but that we should obey Him from the heart and by our obedience experience His love in a deeper way. Remember that Christian love is an act of the will. Just as parents and children grow in their love for each other, so the Father wants to have a closer relationship with us. He wants us to come nearer and go deeper. Christians know that God is their Father, but we don't always allow Him *to be a Father to us*. I recall times when my wife and I planned special days for our children, but they had their own plans, and we let them have their way. Then they would find out what they had missed and regretted it. God wants to be a Father to us (2 Corinthians 6:14–7:1), but we have our own plans and miss opportunities for deeper love.

The Fellowship of the Holy Spirit

The Father loves us so much that He sent His Son to die for us, and the Son loves us so much that He willingly laid down his life for our sins on the cross. But the Holy Spirit loves us so much that *He is willing to live in us and be our helper.* Jesus was away from heaven for about thirty-three years, but the Spirit has been dwelling in the church here on earth for centuries. I'm not suggesting that the Spirit loves us more than the Father and the Son do, but I do thank the Spirit for His longsuffering with me and for His forgiveness when I have grieved Him. I want to "keep in step with the Spirit" (Galatians 5:25) and allow Him to work out God's will in my life. Living with me takes love!

The ministry of the Holy Spirit is to glorify the Son. "He will bring glory to me," said Jesus, "by taking from what is mine and making it known to you" (John 16:14). As He reveals Jesus to us in the Word, we love the Savior more and grow in our obedience to Him and thereby glorify Him. The Holy Spirit doesn't work in spite of us or instead of us; He works in us and through us, and we must be fit vessels for Him to fill and use.

The Greek word translated "fellowship" (*koinonia*) has become popular among believers in recent years. I hear of *koinonia* Sunday school classes, youth groups, camps and retreats, and even coffee bars. The word simply means, "to have in common," but this "having in common" means much more than being the same age or enjoying the same blend of coffee. No matter what your age or gender, your income or education, your hobbies or political views, if you know Jesus as your Savior and Lord, you and I can enjoy fellowship because the Spirit is living within us. We have Jesus in common, and the Spirit witnesses to that fact. If the basis of our fellowship is something other than Jesus as revealed by the Spirit in the Word—perhaps a pet doctrine, a favorite translation, a gifted teacher, a denominational distinctive—then it is not true *koinonia*.

How do we "keep in step with the Spirit" and experience this deeper fellowship? For one thing, we must cooperate with the Spirit in His main ministry, which is glorifying Jesus Christ. Jesus came to glorify the Father, and the Spirit came to glorify the Son. The

Spirit seeks no glory for Himself, nor should we. "I eagerly expect and hope that I will in no way be ashamed, but will have sufficient courage so that now as always Christ will be exalted in my body, whether by life or by death. For to me, to live is Christ and to die is gain" (Philippians 1:20–21). Life is what we are alive to, and Christians are alive to Christ because they are alive in Christ.

Glorifying Jesus Christ is the major ministry of the Spirit, and He accomplishes that by making God's people more like Christ. The Spirit wrote the Word to reveal Jesus, and as we learn the Word and obey it, we see Jesus and become more like Him (2 Corinthians 3:18). If we ignore the Bible, the book the Spirit wrote for us, we grieve the Spirit and miss the help He wants to give us. "But his delight is in the law of the Lord, and on his law he meditates day and night" (Psalm 1:2).

The Spirit not only glorifies the Lord and teaches us the Bible, but He is also working with Jesus in building the church on the earth. Whenever sinners turn to Jesus and are saved, the Spirit baptizes them into the body of Christ and gives them gifts for serving Christ and building up His body (1 Corinthians 12:1–13). If I separate myself from God's people and fail to use my spiritual gifts to minister to the church, I am grieving the Holy Spirit. To "keep in step with the Spirit" means witnessing to the lost and ministering to the saints to the glory of God, and for this we need the Holy Spirit (John 15:26–27). Let's not so emphasize the spectacular gifts of the Spirit that we forget the practical graces of the Spirit, what Paul called "the fruit of the Spirit" (Galatians 5:22–23).

As God's children, we are a privileged people, but with every privilege, there also comes danger.

A Trinity of Perils

Let's turn our attention to some New Testament churches and discover how they "fell" from the blessing of God because they ignored their privileges.

The Galatian Churches: Falling from Grace (Galatians 5:4)

The Judaizers (legalistic teachers) who hounded Paul had invaded the churches he founded in Galatia and had begun to lead the new believers astray. The Christians were moving away from the gospel as they tried to mix God's grace through Jesus Christ with the law of Moses, and this was causing all kinds of problems. "You who are trying to be justified by law have been alienated from Christ; you have fallen away from grace" (Galatians 5:4). These Gentile believers had never worn the yoke of the Jewish law, yet here they were, stepping out of Christian freedom into legalistic slavery (Galatians 5:1). They had all the wealth of Christ at their disposal and were now abandoning it to go into debt to the law of Moses (Galatians 5:2–6). They had been "running a good race" but were now going in the wrong direction (Galatians 5:7–12).

The Christian life must be a balanced life. We aren't saved by keeping the law, but neither are we lawless in the way we live. We aren't saved by good works, but our salvation leads to good works that are evidence that we know Jesus. It's a dangerous thing to get out of balance. Some churches take grace to an extreme and turn liberty into license. "They are godless men, who change the grace of our God into a license for immorality and deny Jesus Christ our only Sovereign and Lord" (Jude 4). "They claim to know God, but by their actions they deny him" (Titus 1:16). The Galatian churches went to the other extreme: they so emphasized law that they forgot the grace of God. They had fallen out of the sphere of grace and were in bondage to a religious system that made them slaves.

Paul pointed out that under the law of Moses the people were treated like children. They were under rules and regulations and subjected to "babysitters" who enforced those rules. But in Jesus Christ, we have an adult standing with God and the privilege of drawing upon His wealth (Galatians 4:1–7). The Spirit lives within us and gives us the direction and dynamic we need to live for

Christ. It's a basic theological truth that law brings out the worst in us while grace brings out the best in us. The old nature knows no law, but the new nature needs no law. The motivation for obedience comes from our hearts, where "the love of God has been poured out" (Romans 5:5).

When churches fall from grace, the pulpit becomes harsh and demanding, and those who preach threaten instead of "speaking the truth in love" (Ephesians 4:15). When we magnify the law, we demand the impossible, because "the law made nothing perfect" (Hebrews 7:19). When we magnify the grace of Jesus Christ, we encourage holy living, for it's only by grace that we serve Jesus Christ. "But by the grace of God I am what I am," wrote Paul (1 Corinthians 15:10), and that's the testimony of every true Christian who walks in the Spirit. God's holy law reveals His righteousness and His will for us, and God's wonderful grace provides what we need to obey Him and live a holy life.

The Ephesian Church: Falling from Love (Revelation 2:1–7)

If we had visited the congregation at Ephesus and worshiped with them, we would have admired everything they were doing. The members were hard workers and were always busy. They didn't tolerate false doctrine, and when they detected heretics, they dealt with them. In spite of opposition and difficulties, they kept right on going and never considered quitting. In every way, the church at Ephesus appeared to be a successful church.

"Man looks at the outward appearance, but the Lord looks at the heart" (1 Samuel 16:7), and when the Lord looked at the hearts of the Ephesian believers, He saw that they were not filled with God's love. The verdict was, "You have forsaken your first love" (Revelation 2:4), and the word translated *forsaken* also means "to neglect" and even "to divorce." The honeymoon was over (Jeremiah 2:1–2), and the Ephesians' love for Christ and for one another had cooled. The Lord isn't necessarily pleased with us just because we are busy serving in the church, and we can't evaluate a congregation just by its outward activities. If our service and sacrifices are not motivated by love, the Lord can't accept and bless them.

"Remember the height from which you are fallen!" the Lord warned them (Revelation 2:5). The church members thought they were "on top of everything," but they were wrong. Paul had founded the church and taught them the Word, and Timothy had taken over when Paul left. Tradition tells us that the apostle John also ministered in Ephesus. The church had received three inspired letters from Paul—Ephesians, 1 Timothy, and 2 Timothy—and Paul had privately exhorted the Ephesian elders (Acts 20:13–38). What a privileged church it was! In the Ephesian epistle, Paul had pointed out the heights of the Christian life that we enjoy as we sit enthroned with Christ in the heavenly places, but now the Ephesians had fallen from those heights because their love for Christ had grown cold.

Great privileges are no guarantee of great devotion to Jesus. When the Lord Jesus restored Peter to discipleship (John 21), He didn't ask about his theology or his ministry methods. Three times Jesus asked, "Do you love me?" If the servant doesn't love the Master, then the service will not please the Master or receive His blessing and reward. "For Christ's love compels us," wrote Paul (2 Corinthians 5:14), and that's the only motivation the Lord will accept. The Lord looks on the heart and wants to see it filled with love, "honeymoon love," that grows deeper and deeper as the years go by. In his Ephesian epistle, Paul urged the believers to "do the will of God from your heart" (Ephesians 6:6). The prophet Jonah finally obeyed God and preached God's message in Nineveh, but he didn't do it from his heart. In fact, he hated the people he preached to and was angry with the Lord.

It's a wonderful thing for a local church family and staff to be busy for the Lord, but no amount of religious activity can substitute for our love for Jesus Christ. Martha was busy serving Jesus,

but it was Mary whom Jesus commended, because she took time
to love Him and listen to His Word (Luke 10:38–42). Jesus still
asks us as He asked Peter, "Do you love me?"

The Corinthian Church: Falling from the Spirit's Fellowship

Whenever one of my students said, "We need to be more like the
churches in the New Testament," I would ask, "Which one would
you want to be like?" The class would then discuss some of the
problems in these churches. The believers in Rome were divided over diets and holy days, and the members of the churches in
Galatia were "biting and devouring each other" (Galatians 5:15).
Two women in Philippi disagreed over something and created a
serious problem (Philippians 4:2–3). The Colossian church was
mixed up in Jewish legalism and Oriental mysticism and asceti-
cism, and some of the saints in Thessalonica had quit their jobs
and expected the church to care for them as they eagerly awaited
the Lord's return.

And then there was Corinth. The congregation was split four
ways (1 Corinthians 1:11), and some of the believers were using
their spiritual gifts to show off instead of to serve the church. Ri-
valry and confusion characterized their worship services, and people even got drunk at the church's "love feasts." The members were
suing one another in the public courts, and if that weren't enough,
one church member was openly committing fornication with his
stepmother—and some believers were proud that their church
leaders were "so loving and tolerant."

What was the cause of such shameful behavior on the part
of these professed believers in Jesus Christ? Paul pointed out the
cause in the first two chapters of his first letter: they were depending on "the wisdom of the world" and not on the wisdom that
comes from God as the Spirit teaches the Word. When you starting thinking like the world, you soon start living like the world,
a tragedy that is occurring in churches today. Instead of building

the ministry on the "gold, silver and costly stones" found in God's Word (Proverbs 2:1–3; 3:13–15; 8:10–11, 17–21), the Corinthians were using "wood, hay and straw," cheap materials you can easily pick up in a vacant lot. If you want gold, silver, and costly stones—the enduring wealth of God's wisdom—you have to dig for them. God help those church leaders who are too lazy to seek the Lord and dig into His Word but settle for whatever they can "pick up" out in the world!

The Corinthians were not rightly related to the Holy Spirit; they were not making "every effort to maintain the unity of the Spirit through the bond of peace" (Ephesians 4:3). Paul called them "worldly—mere infants in Christ" (1 Corinthians 3:1–3). The Greek word translated *worldly* in the NIV means "made of flesh." (The KJV uses the word *carnal*.) The Christians in Corinth were living by the standards and appetites of the old life and were not walking in the Spirit. They were feeding on the world's trash and not growing in the Lord. They needed to obey the Holy Spirit, who is referred to more than fifty times in the two Corinthian letters.

The Corinthian Christians were "enriched in every way" in the gifts of the Spirit (1 Corinthians 1:5), but they were sadly deficient in demonstrating the graces of the Spirit, such as love and peace and self-control. They simply were not spiritual Christians. They lived to please their own appetites, and they lived just like the lost people in the world. When their church leaders came together, they didn't search the Scriptures or pray for spiritual wisdom. Instead, they shared the cheap ideas they borrowed from the world and made decisions that catered to satisfying the old sinful nature. Their worship services didn't glorify the Lord because there was no evidence that the Spirit was at work.

I once heard A. W. Tozer say, "If God were to take the Holy Spirit out of this world, most of what the church is doing would go right on and nobody would know the difference." What an indictment—yet I believe it is true. Unwilling to pay the price to be maturing spiritual believers, many church members depend on worldly wisdom and fleshly energy to attempt to accomplish the work of the Lord, and it will not work. Scottish author George MacDonald wrote, "In whatever man does without God, he must fail miserably or *succeed more miserably.*" A church that is successful in the eyes of men may be a failure in the eyes of God. If you doubt that, read Revelation 2–3.

If we expect the Holy Spirit to work in and through our churches, we must seek above all else to glorify Jesus Christ, for that is one reason the Spirit was sent (John 16:14). The Corinthians argued over who was the greatest—Paul, Peter, or Apollos— and a "super-spiritual" group rejected all human leadership and claimed to follow only Christ. They probably caused more trouble than the other three groups combined!

Thomas Merton wrote, "The most dangerous man in the world is the contemplative who is guided by nobody. He trusts his own visions. He obeys the attraction of an interior voice but will not listen to other men. He identifies the will of God with anything that makes him feel, within his own heart, a big, warm, sweet interior glow . . . [S]uch a man can wreck a whole city . . . or even a nation."[6]

For the word *contemplative,* substitute pastor, board chairman, missionary, committee member, or parachurch executive, and it still applies. No matter how large or affluent a ministry may be, if the leaders are not searching the Scriptures for God's wisdom, praying for God's guidance and power, and seeking to glorify God's Son, their work is in vain, for the Spirit is not in control. At the judgment seat of Christ, the wood, hay, and straw will only burn up.

St. Patrick said, "I bind unto myself today the strong Name of the Trinity." It is a strong name, and it is a name we can trust.

And John Newton wrote:

May the grace of Christ our Savior
And the Father's boundless love

With the Holy Spirit's favor,
Rest upon us from above.

Thus may we abide in union
With each other and the Lord,
And possess, in sweet communion,
Joys which earth cannot afford.

CHAPTER 4

THE SPIRITUAL LEADER'S BENEDICTION

Now I commit you to God and to the word of his grace, which can build you up and give you an inheritance among all those who are sanctified (Acts 20:32).

I'M GRATEFUL TO the Lord for the Christian friends who have taught me, encouraged me, and prayed for me since I began my ministry in 1950. As I get older, their number keeps decreasing as one by one they go to be with the Lord. But I'm finding it difficult to find people to replace them. I can identify with those Ephesian elders who heard their dear friend (and former pastor) Paul say, "You will never see my face again." To encourage their hearts, and the hearts of all Christians who have had to say goodbye to ministering friends, Paul spoke the words of this benediction.

The overseers of the church at Ephesus had traveled for perhaps thirty miles to meet the apostle at Miletus. Paul was in a hurry to get to Jerusalem to deliver a special offering, but he paused long enough to minister one more time to some of the leaders who had served with him during his three years in Ephesus. In his message, Paul first reviewed the past and described his ministry among them (Acts 20:18–21). He then explained his present situation (vv. 22–27) and concluded with some warnings about future dangers (vv. 28–35). The meeting concluded with a tearful farewell as Paul boarded ship and sailed away.

On a number of occasions I've had to say farewell to people I ministered to and with, not knowing if we would ever meet again in this world. Of course, today we have cell phones, fax machines, and e-mail, all of which can give us almost immediate contact with people in many parts of the world, but Paul and his friends didn't have those devices. His next meeting with these elders would be in heaven. He could pray for them and write to them, but he would no longer be there in person to minister to them and help them deal with church problems.

However, though Paul departed, his benediction in verse 32 gave them four assurances that could keep them going in a triumphant life of service for the Lord. If changes disappoint and distress us, we can keep on serving the Lord effectively because of these assurances.

THE LORD GUARDS HIS CHURCH

AMONG JOHN WESLEY's dying words were, "The best of all—God is with us." God may change His workers, but His work goes right on. We are not the disciples of human preachers and teachers but of the Lord Jesus Christ. He is the head of His church, and He works through His servants to build the church. Prayer partners, friends in "life groups," pastors, and teachers can all contribute to our spiritual growth, but ultimately it's the Lord who does the work. Let's appreciate friends and thank God for them, but let's not become so dependent on the servants that we neglect the Master. There's no place in the Christian life for that kind of co-dependence.

The verb Paul used is encouraging: "I commit you to God." It means "to entrust for safekeeping." The great temple to Diana in Ephesus was not only a religious shrine but also a bank where people could deposit their valuables for protection, and the elders knew this. But the temple isn't there today, because buildings made by human hands are not enduring. When Paul committed his friends to the Lord, he was putting them into the hands of a Friend who could not fail. "Lord, you have been our dwelling place throughout all generations" (Psalm 90:1). Moses wrote those words, and the biblical record indicates that during his lifetime Moses lived in more than forty different places. My wife and I have had addresses in Indiana, Illinois, Wisconsin, Kentucky, and Nebraska, but like Moses, our spiritual address has always been the same—the Lord God Almighty.

Believers dwell "in the shelter of the Most High" and "in the shadow of the Almighty" (Psalm 91:1). A shadow might not seem to be a good place of refuge, but when it represents the presence of Almighty God, it's the safest place in the world. "The Lord Almighty is with us; the God of Jacob is our fortress" (Psalm 46:7). The world around us may quickly change and threaten us, but we have nothing to fear. "If God is for us, who can be against us?" (Romans 8:31).

When Christian people leave us and things start to change in our lives, we usually get a feeling of insecurity, and insecurity often leads to fear. Faith and fear can't live in the same heart, and if our eyes are fixed on the circumstances around us, they can't be fixed on Jesus (Hebrews 12:2). Jesus asks us as He asked His disciples, "You of little faith, why are you so   afraid?" (Matthew 8:26). Why are we afraid? Because we've forgotten the wonderful security we have in the Lord.

"And surely I am with you always, to the very end of the age" (Matthew 28:20). No other friend can give you a promise like that.

The Lord Teaches His Church

During his ministry in Ephesus, Paul had committed the Word to the believers there, but now he was committing them to the Word. We who are "in Christ" also need to be "in the Word," and the Word must be in us (Colossians 3:16). When we rely on the Word of God and act upon it, the Holy Spirit takes over in our lives and God's promises are fulfilled. Jesus, the living Word, embraces us and transforms us through the Scriptures, and that Word gives us all that we need for life and service.

Those who serve the Lord and His church should learn everything they can that will help them serve better, and at the top of the list is a deepening knowledge of the Word of God. I'm concerned about people who claim they have read the current Christian bestsellers but have never yet read the entire Bible or carefully studied one major book in the Bible. God's workers are equipped by knowing God's Word (2 Timothy 3:16–17), and this Word is adequate for every experience of life (2 Peter 1:1–4). The psalmist wrote, "Your statutes are forever right; give me understanding that I may live" (Psalm 119:144).

Paul used a special name for the Scriptures: "the word of his grace." The Bible is the bankbook that records the riches of God's grace (Ephesians 2:7; 3:14–21). If I want to know how wealthy I am in Christ, I need only to read God's Word and note what He has done for me and what He promises to do for me. He is "the God of all grace" (1 Peter 5:10), who joyfully and generously provides our needs when we ask at the throne of grace. Some of us are so pleased with ourselves and our own achievements that we fail to understand how bankrupt we really are (Revelation 3:14–22).

It's unfortunate that too many Christians view the Bible as only a book of rules, a compendium of laws and limitations, when its major message is the marvelous liberating grace of God. The same God who shows us our own spiritual poverty also makes available His unlimited spiritual riches, for God has "blessed us in the heavenly realms with every spiritual blessing in Christ" (Ephesians 1:3). After reviewing the demands of the Christian life, Paul asked, "And who is equal to such a task?" (2 Corinthians 2:16). He answered his own question: "Not that we are competent in ourselves to claim anything for ourselves, but our competence comes from God" (2 Corinthians 3:5). That's grace!

The Bible is God's gracious gift to His people. "The Bible is alive; it speaks to me," said Martin Luther. "It has feet; it runs after me. It has hands; it lays hold on me." How gracious of God to give us such a book. The Spirit of grace teaches us the "word of his grace" so that we can grow day by day. "But his delight is in the law of the Lord, and on his law he meditates day and night" (Psalm 1:2). God's Word gives us the wisdom we need to understand ourselves, other people, and the situations of life, but it also gives us the faith we need to obey the Lord's will. The Bible is the indispensable book that never fails to teach us if we study it with hearts prepared to obey the Lord.

THE LORD BUILDS HIS CHURCH

"I WILL BUILD MY CHURCH," Jesus said to His disciples, "and the gates of Hades will not overcome it" (Matthew 16:18). How many times it has seemed to us that the work of the Lord was destroyed in some part of the world, only to discover years later that the roots of the church had gone deeper and the ministry had become more fruitful. I was a seminary student in the early 1950s when Christian missionaries were expelled from China, and I recall hearing one of the missionaries speak in a chapel. She described what happened to the congregations, the leaders, and the property and painted a depressing picture. But look at the church in China today. Millions have trusted Jesus Christ, and churches are multiplying. During World War II, Mussolini ordered all Christian missionaries to leave Ethiopia, but when they returned after the war, they discovered a strong, thriving church.

Jesus builds His church by gifting individual believers who, in turn, help to build others in the faith. One of Paul's favorite metaphors is that of building or, as some translations have it, edifying. The word is used at least twenty-five times in Acts and in Paul's epistles. The Lord gives spiritual gifts to His people so that we may serve one another and build up the body of Christ (Ephesians 4:11–13). Whatever is done in the Christian assembly "must be done for strengthening of the church" (1 Corinthians 14:26). We wonder how much "spiritual building" results from shallow preaching, worldly music, and "religious entertainment" that appeal to many Christians today. Sometimes the sanctuary becomes a theater, and the goal is to send people home feeling good. But James 4:7–10 is still in the Bible, and we need to take it to heart.

This spiritual building process requires that believers cooperate with the Lord. He builds us up through His Word, but His command to us is "build yourselves up in your most holy faith and pray in the Holy Spirit" (Jude 20). We are "living stones" in the holy temple of the Lord (1 Peter 2:4–6), and we want to submit to the Lord and let Him use us as He desires. Dead bricks can't resist the mason, but "living stones" can resist the Lord and weaken the structure. Of course, they do it to their own hurt and to the hurt of others, for a stone out of place becomes a stumbling block. It takes little ability to tear something down, and there are people who go from church to church leaving wreckage behind. Paul warns us, "If anyone destroys God's temple, God will destroy him" (1 Corinthians 3:17). Ominous words indeed! Today, Jesus is gathering and building, but Satan is destroying and scattering. For whom are we working?

THE LORD REWARDS HIS CHURCH

ALL WHO HAVE been saved through faith in Jesus Christ are "sanctified" by the Lord and set apart for His enjoyment and employment. We are also "heirs of God and co-heirs with Christ" (Romans 8:17), and the Holy Spirit of God is the guarantee and seal that our God-given inheritance is secure (Ephesians 1:14). We can draw upon our spiritual riches today (Ephesians 1:3) and look forward to enjoying God's glorious riches forever in heaven (Colossians 1:12; 3:24). Because we have been justified by His grace, we are God's heirs and have the "hope of eternal life" in glory (Titus 3:7). We have been born again "into an inheritance that can never perish, spoil or fade" (1 Peter 1:4). What a future we have in Jesus!

Knowing that we have this glorious future, we seek to serve and obey the Lord today. After all, God has paid a great price to make us His own, and He claims us as His inheritance (Ephesians 1:18). It is love for Christ, not a desire for rewards, that is our deepest motive for obedience, but the Lord in His generosity rewards us for faithful service. Jesus said, "Look, I am coming soon! My reward is with me, and I will give to everyone according to what they have done" (Rev. 22:12 TNIV). Charles Spurgeon said, "There will be no crown-wearers in heaven that were not cross-bearers on earth."

It isn't easy to serve as a spiritual leader in a local church. After naming some of the many difficulties and hazards of his own ministry, Paul climaxed the list by adding, "Besides everything else, I face daily the pressure of my concern for all the churches" (2 Corinthians 11:28). The external trials he listed were insignificant in light of the inner pressures and burdens Paul felt as he shepherded the flocks. The servants of Jesus Christ are sometimes misunderstood and unjustly criticized; they are frequently taken for granted and not always thanked for what they do; and they and their loved ones are open to attack by the devil and his demonic forces. But the true servants don't complain but give thanks that they can share "the fellowship of sharing in [Christ's] sufferings" (Philippians 3:10).

A godly pastor friend, now in heaven, used to remind me, "You can't receive your reward twice. If you get your reward here, you won't get it in heaven." He was referring, of course, to the words of Jesus in Matthew 6:1–18. Leaders receive much more of the blame and much less of the credit, but this doesn't discourage them as long as Jesus gets the glory.

Paul's letter to the Ephesian church was written probably three or four years after his meeting with the elders at Miletus, recorded in Acts 20. I suggest you read the letter carefully at one sitting and see how these four assurances are woven into Paul's inspired words. Then, go back to your ministry with encouragement and joy, thanking the Lord for the privilege you have of being a servant of Jesus Christ.

CHAPTER 5

THE BENEDICTION OF UNITY

May the God who gives endurance and encouragement give you a spirit of unity among yourselves as you follow Christ Jesus, so that with one heart and mouth you may glorify the God and Father of our Lord Jesus Christ (Romans 15:5–6).

YOU EXPECT TO FIND a benediction near the close of a letter, but Paul wrote this one near the end of a long section in Romans that focuses on unity in the church (Romans 14:1–15:13). As he dictated his letter, Paul dropped in these benedictions because he wanted his readers—and that includes us—to share in the blessings he was writing about. In this case it's the blessing of unity among believers.

The problem in the churches in Rome arose because the congregations included both Jewish and Gentile believers. Some of the believers were weak in their faith and didn't understand the freedom they had in Christ. The Jews in particular had a difficult time moving away from the traditions that had been so meaningful to them. They thought they had to maintain kosher homes and follow the Jewish religious calendar in order to please God.

Other believers in the church were strong in the faith and understood that Christians no longer had to obey the dietary regulations and the observance of special days, so they enjoyed their freedom in Jesus Christ. Of course, the Gentiles had never been under the Mosaic law, so the traditions meant little to them. There were bad feelings between the two groups. The stronger members looked with disdain on the weaker ones, and the weaker believers judged and condemned the stronger members, and the situation weakened the witness of the church.

Paul's solution to the problem points the way to the healing of divisions among God's people. He gives us three instructions to obey: accept one another in Christ (14:1–12), build one another up in Christ (14:13–23), and seek to please one another for the sake of Christ (15:1–7). Christ is the head of the church and the heart of its fellowship, and we have no right to reject those whom God has received. Paul opens and closes this discussion with the admonition to be accepting of one another (14:1; 15:7). We can't ignore it.

The benediction stands at the close of Paul's third admonition, and it presents the spiritual truths that enable us to receive strength to obey his instructions. "Am I supposed to set aside the law of God?" asks the weaker believer. "I won't do it!"

And the strong believer says, "Jesus died to set me free, and I will never forfeit the liberty I have in Christ!" To both groups, Paul explains the truths involved in building unity among the people of God. Unity isn't based on things cultural, national, or organizational, but on things spiritual. No matter what our background, our position in Jesus Christ makes us new creatures, and this means we have a new relationship to one another.

UNITY COMES FROM GOD

UNITY IS NOT UNIFORMITY. Unity is diversity held together by love and truth. When the choir sings in unison, the sound is lovely, but when it sings in parts, the sound is much more beautiful. A garden of one variety of roses would be fragrant and beautiful, but a many-colored rose garden would be even more beautiful, and if you planted a variety of flowers with the roses, the results would be stunning. During our ministry travels, my wife and I have occasionally visited famous gardens, from acres of tulips in Holland to the world-famous Buchardt Gardens in British Columbia, and it is diversity and not uniformity that caught our attention. Our God is infinitely original.

The church of Jesus Christ encourages unity, not uniformity. We aren't held together by external laws but by internal life, love, and truth. We come from diverse backgrounds, but in Christ there is unity in diversity. "There is neither Jew now Greek, slave nor free, male nor female, for you are all one in Christ Jesus" (Galatians 3:28). Eugene Peterson has caught the spirit of our benediction in his paraphrase of Romans 15:5–6 in *The Message:* "May our dependably steady and warmly personal God develop maturity in you so that you get along with each other as well as Jesus gets along with us all. Then we'll be a choir—not our voices only, but our lives singing in harmony in a stunning anthem to the God and Father of our Master Jesus!"

Unity isn't something we work up, like cheerleaders at a football game. Unity is a blessing that God sends down through His Holy Spirit. Psalm 133 describes it this way:

How good and pleasant it is
    when brothers live together in unity!
It is like precious oil poured on the head,
    running down on the beard,
running down on Aaron's beard,
    down upon the collar of his robes.
It is as if the dew of Hermon
    were falling on Mount Zion.
For there the Lord bestows his blessing,
    even life forevermore.

Both oil and dew are symbols of the Holy Spirit. The oil runs off Aaron's beard *and bathes the precious stones on the breastplate and makes them one.* These stones represent the twelve tribes of Israel who are one in the Lord—unity in diversity. The dew helps to produce the fruitfulness of the soil, and the Spirit helps to produce the fruitfulness of the soul. Where there is true spiritual unity there will be the beautiful fruit of the Spirit.

Through the Holy Spirit, God gives us endurance and encouragement, just the qualities we need if we are going to promote unity in the church. Instead of getting angry and leaving the fellowship, we bear with the failings of others—and they bear with ours. Instead of criticizing and exposing the faults of the saints, we encourage God's people and cover their faults with Christian love. This helps them to mature—and they help us to mature. "Bear with each other and forgive whatever grievances you may have against one another. Forgive as the Lord forgave you" (Colossians 3:13).

Only God can supply that "spirit of unity among ourselves" that binds us together as the children of God. When we confess our sins and forsake them, when we stop criticizing and gossiping about one another, and when we pray for one another and sincerely seek to serve one another, then the spirit of unity will come and bring us together as one beautiful choir or garden. Then there will be unity in diversity, and God will be glorified in the variety and the unity of the people and ministries that emerge. But for this miracle to happen, we must humble ourselves and pray and sincerely obey Ephesians 4:3—"Make every effort to keep the unity of the Spirit through the bond of peace."

Unity Centers in Christ

THE PHRASE "as you follow Christ" lays down a personal condition that we dare not ignore. Weymouth translates it "in accordance with the standard Christ Jesus sets." While we ask the Father for endurance, encouragement, and a spirit of unity, we must also obey what He says and follow close to the Savior. Unity is a by-product of a faithful discipleship, for if all of us are following the same Master, we will be walking together and moving in the same direction. The major ministry of the Holy Spirit is to glorify Christ (John 16:14), so if we all seek to honor Jesus, the Spirit will bring us together in glorifying Him, "so that in everything he might have the supremacy" (Colossians 1:18).

Years ago, A. W. Tozer warned us about the "fan-club mentality" that was taking over in churches. An examination of the advertisements in almost any current Christian magazine makes us question at times whether Jesus Christ is given the place of pre-eminence, and sometimes it appears that the "fan-club mentality" has almost taken over.

The Father has but one gift to give His people, and that gift is His Son. No other gift is necessary, because everything we need is in Christ. When gifted men and woman take the place that belongs only to Jesus, the Spirit is grieved, because the Spirit's ministry is to glorify Christ. The result is that the church is divided and the ministry is hindered. Paul says it well in 1 Corinthians 1:27–31:

> But God chose the foolish things of the world to shame the wise; God chose the weak things of the world to shame the strong. He chose the lowly things of this world and the de-spised things—and the things that are not—to nullify the things that are, so that no one may boast before him. It is because of him that you are in Christ Jesus, who has become for us wisdom from God—that is, our righteousness, holi-ness and redemption. Therefore, as it is written: "Let him who boasts boast in the Lord."

The Christian who diligently reads the Bible and trusts the Spirit to open up its truths will discover the fullness of Christ to meet every need. Jesus is adequate for every need and situation. Paul wrote his epistle to the Romans from Corinth, where he was trying to help that church face and solve its many problems, and his solution was simply Jesus Christ. Once we begin to focus on human leaders and magnify them, we lose access to everything we have in Christ, and we get only what fallen humanity can give to us. When Christ is the center of our worship and fellowship and when He alone is glorified, there will be unity among God's people and adequacy for God's workers.

This is what Jesus prayed for: "I have given them the glory that you gave me, that they may be one as we are one" (John 17:22). When His glory is revealed through us, His people will be united before a broken world, and lost sinners will see what heavenly oneness really is. Unity isn't manufactured; the Spirit ministers it to us.

Unity Begins in the Heart

UNITY MEANS WORSHIPING and serving the Lord "with one heart." Diversity is not transformed into unity by dynamic leadership, clever slogans and promotion, or any other merchandising technique. Diversity is transformed into unity when our hearts fully belong to Jesus Christ, when we love and obey Him and want to glorify Him above everything else. There is a false unity that is manufactured by pressure from without, but what the church needs to manifest is the true unity that is produced by spiritual power and passion from within. This is the work of the Spirit.

I was scheduled to speak in Germany at the annual conference of an international mission. A few days before we left, one of the leaders phoned me and confided that there was a serious division among the leaders, partly doctrinal and partly organizational. Immediately my wife and I began to pray with them for the Spirit to work in hearts and bring about unity. When we arrived, the director of the mission informed us that God had won the victory at a prayer meeting when the missionaries were broken and humbled before the Lord and each other. Everything came into focus, they saw that attitudes had been selfish, and the Lord gave them blessed unity. Needless to say, we had a glorious conference.

When God's people have "one heart," this doesn't mean they agree on every detail of every decision. It means they all have one goal in mind: to glorify Jesus Christ. In managing the affairs of a ministry, I may have one view of a situation and you may have another view, but our purpose is not to solve a problem but to honor Jesus Christ. Prayer, patience, the promises of the Word, and the love of the Spirit will prepare us to examine the matter and make the right decisions.

Division begins with selfish desires that sometimes are hidden in "pious" prayer requests that are based on wrong motives (James 4:1–3). Lot's craving for land and wealth separated him from his godly uncle, Abraham. Achan's selfish desires for wealth brought defeat to Israel. Ananias and Sapphira's selfish desire to be honored as spiritual people cost them their lives. Even the apostles had arguments over which of them was the greatest, and Jesus had to rebuke them. A godly pastor, now in heaven, occasionally reminded me that the only thing the Bible said is "great" about the human family is its wickedness (Genesis 6:5)!

If I cultivate a divided heart, I will soon have a divided and unstable life and ministry (James 1:8). If I insist on having my way, people will start taking sides, and the division will deepen and expand. The heart of every problem is the problem in the heart, and until we honestly start dealing with heart attitudes, the problem will never be solved. Even esteemed leaders like Peter and Barnabas can be wrong at times, as Paul points out in Galatians 2, where he opposes Peter's hypocritical separation from the Gentiles. On two occasions Joshua trusted his own heart instead of seeking the Lord's guidance, and the results were painful and embarrassing (Joshua 7, 9). King Solomon's heart was divided between his love for the Lord and his love for his foreign wives and their false gods, and this eventually led to a divided kingdom. Yet it was Solomon who wrote, "Above all else, guard your heart, for it is the wellspring of life" (Proverbs 4:23).

Unity Is Expressed Openly

WHEN THE HEARTS of God's people are united in the Lord, their worship and conversation will be Spirit led, and their words will glorify God. Yet how many times has a congregation courageously sung the words from the hymn "Onward Christian Soldiers," "We are not divided, all one body we," when they *are* divided. Some Christians silence their consciences by talking about an "invisible church" that is perfectly united, and they forget that Jesus prayed that the church would demonstrate its divine oneness *visibly* to a watching world (John 17:13–23). Jesus was crucified in a place so crowded and cosmopolitan that Pilate had to use three different languages to declare His crime, and yet we use the concept of an "invisible church"—true as it may be—to defend our disunity before a broken world seeking healing.

Too often people use the gift of speech to promote themselves instead of to glorify the Lord. Not only what we say, but how we say it, can unite people to the Lord or turn them away in disgust. Abraham's words to Lot saved the family from a painful division (Genesis 13), as did Gideon's words to the proud men of Ephraim (Judges 8:1–4). "Let your conversation be always full of grace, seasoned with salt, so that you may know how to answer everyone" (Colossians 4:6). No wonder Paul warned the believers in Colosse against sins of the tongue, such as "anger, rage, malice, slander, and filthy language from your lips" (Colossians 3:8).

In the verses that follow this benediction in Romans 15 (7–12), Paul describes a great choir of both Jews and Gentiles praising the Lord with one mouth. First, the believing Jews praise God among the Gentiles, then the Gentiles praise the Lord with the Jews. The middle wall has been broken down (Ephesians 2:11–22), and the temple veil has been torn in two. Indeed, in Jesus Christ, there is no more division. We are all one body, obeying one Master and singing with one voice to His glory.

In recent years, it's been unfortunate that congregational singing has been a cause of division in the churches instead of a means of united witness. One day we shall harmoniously praise God together in heaven, but it wouldn't hurt for us to do some rehearsing while we're awaiting His return. Our singing must be *balanced* ("psalms, hymns and spiritual songs" [Ephesians 5:19]); *biblical* (Colossians 3:16); and always to the glory of the Lord. The proper response to Christian singing should be hearts moved to worship God and not hands moved to applaud the performer.

God will one day judge our words, because what comes out of the mouth is what has been stored away in the heart (Matthew 12:33–37). In his classic chapter on the tongue, James warns us that our words are like sparks from a fire, small in size but great in potential destruction (James 3:5–6). "Consider what a great forest is set on fire by a small spark" (James 3:5). The tongues of the first Christians were set on fire from heaven and their words led to the salvation of three thousand people (Acts 2:3–4, 41), but when the tongue is set on fire from hell, it leads to division and destruction. "Speak when you are angry," wrote Ambrose Bierce, "and you will make the best speech you will ever regret."

Unity Glorifies God

"So WHETHER YOU eat or drink or whatever you do, do it all for the glory of God" (1 Corinthians 10:31). Christians can glorify God by their singing, and it's possible for unbelievers to be brought to the faith just by the witness of Spirit-filled congregational worship (1 Corinthians 14:20–25).

God is glorified when things happen that we can't explain other than by the providence of God. The unity that came to our conference in Germany was the result of God's miraculous intervention. When unexpected funds for ministry arrive just in time, it has to be the work of the Lord, so He alone gets the glory. Dr. Bob Cook used to remind us, "If you can explain what's going on, God didn't do it." Many times I have ministered in churches where God's blessing was evident, but it wasn't because of me, the pastor, the staff or exceptional people in the congregation. It was because everybody wanted the Lord to be glorified. If people go away from church saying, "What a beautiful choir!" or "What an eloquent preacher!" or "What a magnificent sanctuary!" then they are missing the mark. They should go away saying, "What a wonderful Lord they worship!" This means that God alone is receiving the glory.

Jesus made it clear that unity among the children of God is even more important than our public worship. "Therefore, if you are offering your gift at the altar and there remember that your brother has something against you, leave your gift there in front of the altar. First go and be reconciled to your brother; then come and offer your gift" (Matthew 5:23–24). Just before the offering, perhaps we need to add "the act of reconciliation" to our Sunday morning liturgy.

And perhaps we should use Paul's benediction of unity more often to close our services, if only to remind us that unity isn't a luxury—it's a necessity.

CHAPTER 6

THE BENEDICTION OF HOPE

May the God of hope fill you with all joy and peace as you trust in him, so that you may overflow with hope by the power of the Holy Spirit (Romans 15:13).

ACCORDING TO THE APOSTLE PAUL, "faith, hope and love" are the three abiding Christian virtues (1 Corinthians 13:13). Faith compels us to *look up* and have confidence in the true and living God; love constrains us to *look around* and encourage those who need our help; and hope motivates us to *look ahead* with assurance, knowing that the future is our friend because Jesus is our living Lord. As Dr. V. Raymond Edman used to say, "It's always too soon to quit."

Nowhere in the Bible is Christian hope presented as a blind "hope-so" feeling that has no basis in truth. Our hope is in the unchanging Lord and His unfailing promises. It's not in the way we feel or in what people call natural optimism. Because he didn't understand this fact, the cynical American writer H. L. Mencken defined hope as "a pathological belief in the occurrence of the impossible." Abraham would have laughed at that definition. "Against all hope, Abraham in hope believed and so became the father of many nations, just as it had been said to him, 'So shall your offspring be'" (Romans 4:18). Abraham was "fully persuaded that God had power to do what he had promised" (Romans 4:21).

In his poetic *Essay on Man*, Alexander Pope stated pessimistically, "Hope springs eternal in the human breast: Man never is, but always To be Blest." Pope told his friend John Gay never to forget the ninth beatitude: "Blessed is he who expects nothing, for he shall never be disappointed." Neither of Pope's statements is a strong foundation for a life of faith, hope, and love. I prefer the apostle Peter's hymn of joy: "Praise be to the God and Father of our Lord Jesus Christ! In his great mercy he has given us new birth into a living hope through the resurrection of Jesus Christ from the dead" (1 Peter 1:3). When you trust the living word (1 Peter 1:23) of the living Savior, then you have this living hope *plus* the eternal unchanging inheritance that goes with it.

Whenever I hear or read a statement affirming the greatness of ancient Greek civilization, in my own mind I add two qualifications: it was built on slavery, and it offered no one any hope for life after death. That anybody could live or die hopefully was completely unknown in ancient Greek culture, which explains why the philosophers on Mars Hill sneered at Paul's doctrine of the resurrection of the dead (Acts 17:32). The Greek people to whom Paul ministered were "without hope and without God in the world" (Ephesians 2:12). Archeologists uncovered a gravestone in Greece with an epitaph that reads, "I was not—I became—I am not—I care not."

Hope is part of the spiritual energy and vision that keeps us going when everything seems against us. The Bible compares hope to an anchor "firm and secure" (Hebrews 6:18–19). The odd thing about this anchor is that it doesn't go *down* into the depths but reaches up to the heights of heaven where Jesus is, *and nothing can move it.* Furthermore, the anchor "hope" enables us to keep on moving ahead instead of standing still. The Greek philosopher Epictetus wrote, "One must not tie a ship to a single anchor, nor life to a single hope." In spite of that advice, we Christians do tie our lives to a single Hope—"Christ Jesus our hope" (1 Timothy 1:1). Jesus is all we need! Because we love God, we trust Him, and because we trust Him, our hope is strong.

Charles Spurgeon called Romans 15:13 "one of the richest passages in the Word of God,"[7] and the more you ponder it, the more you will agree with him. It describes what it means for

Christian believers to live under the blessing of the benediction of hope.

Living in the Future Tense

We must never forget the past. It would be tragic to have to re-learn the alphabet or the multiplication tables each morning or how to drive a car or cook an egg. We don't live in the past, but if the past doesn't live in us, we are in serious trouble. The past is a rudder to guide us, not an anchor to hold us back. However, if we live only for the present, we will be controlled by "the tyranny of the immediate" and have no future. We learn from the past, we live and work in the present, but we are strongly motivated by the future. As Christians, we live "in the future tense" because the Christian life is a life of promise.

Have you ever met people who are rarely impatient in waiting, who don't complain about circumstances but maintain a bright smile of happy expectancy? People whose outlook is that even if things got worse, they would eventually get better? People who, if they fail or are disappointed, start over again with new expectations? People who see the best in other people and try to encourage them? People who never seem irritated if you interrupt them? No, they aren't graduates of some "positive thinking" course. They are people who live in the future tense, who allow the promised hope in Christ to control their attitudes and actions today. They rest calmly on Jeremiah 29:11: " ' For I know the plans I have for you,' declares the Lord, 'plans to prosper you and not to harm you, plans to give you a hope and a future.' "

No wonder one of Jeremiah's special names for Jehovah was "the Hope of Israel" (14:8; 17:13) and "the hope of their fathers" (50:7).

In his New Testament letters, Paul used the word *hope* fifty-five times as either a noun or a verb, and this includes fourteen references in Romans. D. L. Moody warned about "people who were so heavenly minded they were no earthly good," but that's not what true hope does to us. *True hope enables us to look at earth from heaven's point of view and see the present in the light of the future, and this keeps us going no matter how difficult the circumstances may be.* Whenever we find ourselves looking back with regret or looking around with fear, we have stopped living in the future tense.

The patriarchs set the example for us. "They did not receive the things promised; they only saw them and welcomed them from a distance" (Hebrews 11:13). Abraham didn't look back to Ur of the Chaldees, nor did he look around at Sodom and Gomorrah and the cities of the plains, but he looked ahead to the city of God where he had his eternal citizenship. "For he was looking forward to the city with foundations, whose architect and builder is God" (Hebrews 11:10).

Our God is the God of hope. If we know God and walk with Him, He will brighten our hope so that difficult circumstances and people won't discourage us and take us on costly detours. The opposite of hope is despair, living like "the rest of men, who have no hope" (1 Thessalonians 4:13). Because of God's covenants and promises, we may have hope even in the most difficult of circumstances. For examples of hope in the Lord, consider Joseph waiting in an Egyptian prison, Israel suffering under Egyptian slavery, Joshua facing fierce Canaanite nations, David resolutely waiting for his throne, Jeremiah painfully watching the Jewish nation crumbling around him. Hope works!

The seasons of the year remind us that our God is a God of hope. "If winter comes, can spring be far behind?" asked Shelley in his poem "Ode to the West Wind." Almost every activity of human life is motivated to some degree by hope. Because of hope, farmers plant seeds, teachers instruct students, and people in love get married and have families. Because they anticipate dividends, investors and brokers put money to work. Scientists delve into the complexities of nature because they hope to solve these mysteries and produce practical help for people in need. Life is motivated powerfully by hope. God has made it that way. He arranged that our eyes be in the front of our heads; He wants us to look forward.

When we lay hold of the benediction of hope, we will live in the future tense; this will change the past and the present and make life much more exciting.

Living in the Overflow, Not the Undertow

I grew up near Lake Michigan and often went swimming at Whiting Beach or the Indiana Dunes State Park in the summer. We occasionally saw signs on the beaches that warned BEWARE OF THE UNDERTOW, and I remember how my parents and older siblings made sure I obeyed and stayed in the shallow water. No matter what the water looked like on the surface, the currents deeper down could be much stronger and often ran in the opposite direction. Careless swimmers could suddenly be pulled under and taken out to the deeper water where they might drown.

Life has its undertows, and if we aren't careful, they will pull us under. While Moses was communing with the Lord on Mt. Sinai, an undertow pulled Aaron under, and he pulled the nation with him as together they worshiped a golden idol (Exodus 22). At Kadesh, an unexpected undertow pulled Moses down, and he lost his temper and disobeyed God. This cost him the privilege of entering the Promised Land (Numbers 20:1–13). One quiet evening as King David watched his neighbor's wife bathing, he stepped into an undertow and eventually committed both adultery and murder (2 Samuel 11–12). While actually walking on the water in a storm, Peter stepped into an undertow called unbelief and almost drowned (Matthew 14:22–33). Let those who think they are safe take heed—BEWARE OF THE UNDERTOW!

God's desire for His children is not that we stay in the shallows but that we live in the spiritual overflow that begins in our hearts and gets deeper and deeper. "May the God of hope fill you . . . so that you may overflow." We are channels—not reservoirs—of God's blessing, and we should become deeper and overflow on others so that they may enjoy the Lord.

In preparation for teaching 2 Corinthians at a summer youth camp, I read the epistle over and over again and asked God to give me the emphasis that the teens really needed. As I studied, I couldn't help but notice that Paul used one particular Greek word family over twenty times. It was translated "abound," "overflow," "well up" and "plenty," and I got the impression that Paul wanted us to know that life in the overflow was what the Lord wanted us to enjoy. To be sure, life sometimes overflows with suffering, but then His comfort overflows to meet the need (2 Corinthians 1:5). Look up 2 Corinthians 9:8, memorize it, and ask God to fulfill it in your life.

Today's world is filled with sorrow and battles, but God's grace enables us to overflow with joy and peace. Happiness depends too often on happenings, and God may not always change the circumstances that hurt us; but He will change us and enable us to meet these circumstances joyfully. "I have learned the secret of being content in any and every situation," Paul declared, and then he gave the secret: "I can do everything through him [Christ] who gives me strength" (Philippians 4:12–13). It's good to sing about amazing grace, but it's better to experience abounding grace.

You can go to the supermarket and buy sleep in a medicine form, but you can't buy peace. You can go to a theater and buy entertainment, but you can't purchase joy. Overflowing peace and joy come only to those who claim by faith the benediction blessings of Romans 15:13. King David had been a shepherd in his youth, so he knew how important it was for him to follow the Good Shepherd that we wrote about in Psalm 23. The results? "I shall not be in want" (v. 1), "I will fear no evil" (v. 4), and "my cup overflows" (v. 5). When he looked back, he saw goodness and love following him, and when he looked ahead, he saw the Father's house await-ing him (v. 6). This is the overflowing life!

LiviɳG by FaiᴛH

THE PHRASE "AS YOU TRUST IN HIM" is the key to this overflowing life. The epistle to the Romans is one of three New Testaments books written to explain one verse of Scripture: "The righteous will live by his faith" (Habakkuk 2:4). This verse is quoted in Romans 1:17, Galatians 3:11, and Hebrews 10:38. The epistle to the Romans explains the meaning of "the righteous," Galatians explains "shall live," and Hebrews explains "by faith."

To live by faith means to obey God's Word in spite of the feel-ings within us, the circumstances around us, or the consequences before us. Apply that definition to Abraham offering his son Isaac on Mt. Moriah, to Moses and Israel standing at the Red Sea with the Egyptian army in pursuit, or to Deborah challenging Israel to fight Sisera. Apply it to young David confronting Goliath, to Queen Esther pleading for her people, to the three Hebrew men refusing to worship the idol, or to Jesus facing death on the cross. Then let's apply it to ourselves.

But living by faith in God's Word isn't a popular approach to life. Most people unwittingly follow the advice given by Ralph Waldo Emerson in his famous essay "Self-Reliance": "Trust thyself: every heart vibrates to that iron string." He wrote in his journal, "Self-help is the law of nature." But if nature teaches us anything, it's that we didn't create ourselves and that we cannot live without the help of our creator. Jesus stated it quite clearly, "Apart from me you can do nothing" (John 15:5); Paul wrote, "For it is God who works in you to will and to act according to his good purpose" (Philippians 2:13).

The phrase "as you trust in him" reminds us of what Jesus said to two blind men who cried out for his help: "According to your faith it will be done to you" (Matthew 9:29). Some people have no faith, others have little faith, and a few have great faith. God doesn't work in spite of us or instead of us; He works in and through us to accomplish His will as we step out by faith. The more we trust and obey, the stronger our faith will become, *and the more the Lord will be glorified.* Paul called the Scriptures "the word of faith" (Romans 10:8) because the Word generates faith within us, and that faith is strengthened as we read and meditate on the Scriptures. Said evangelist D. L. Moody, "I used to think I should close my Bible and pray for faith; but I came to see that it was in studying the Word that I was to get faith." Romans 10:17 backs that up: "So faith comes from hearing, and hearing by the word of Christ" (NASB).

Years ago entertainers were singing a popular song called "I Believe" that had unbiblical lyrics. The message was, "Just trust faith, and you can do anything." But Jesus said to His disciples, "Have faith in God" (Mark 11:22), not "Have faith in faith." Faith is only as good as its object. Put faith in yourself, and you will get what human nature can do. Put your faith in money, and you will get what money can do. But put your faith in Almighty God, and you have connected with the greatest power in the universe. If you are doing His will for His glory, He will honor your faith, and you will be singing with Mary: "For the Mighty One has done great things for me—holy is his name" (Luke 1:49).

Living in the Spirit

HOPE, FAITH, JOY, AND PEACE are not blessings we manufacture in our own strength. They are evidences of godly character produced "by the power of the Holy Spirit." Faith (faithfulness), joy, and peace are named among the fruit of the Spirit (Galatians 5:22–23), and it takes time for fruit to mature and reproduce. Fruit must be cultivated, and it has in it the seed for more fruit. Do faith, peace, and joy create the "spiritual climate" in which hope can grow, or is it hope that energizes faith, peace, and joy? Probably both are true, because the graces of the Spirit have a reciprocal ministry. Our faith in the Word increases hope, and faith and hope together help to give us peace and joy. Growing Christians may not be able to analyze and diagram how spiritual nutrition works in the inner person, nor is it necessary that they do so. The important thing is that we yield to the Spirit and allow Him to teach us the Word and help us worship and pray effectively, and the fruit will follow.

Hope begins with salvation. The moment a lost sinner trusts Christ, he or she is justified by faith and receives peace with God. But there is also the gift of hope, for "we rejoice in the hope of the glory of God" (Romans 5:1–2). The children of God have every right to be joyful in the Lord because of the hope they have in Jesus Christ. They no longer need to fear life or death, time or eternity, for birthplace includes a living hope (1 Peter 1:3).

If we are going to mature in the Christian life, we must experience trial and testing, but even these contribute to the brightening of our hope. "Not only so, but we also rejoice in our sufferings, because we know that suffering produces perseverance; perseverance, character; and character, hope. And hope does not disappoint us, because God has poured out his love into our hearts by the Holy Spirit, whom he has given to us" (Romans 5:3–5). *Christians have the privilege of seeing their suffering transformed into Christlike character to the glory of God.* This is the work of the Holy Spirit as we surrender, obey, and wait. The world curses the darkness, but the believer receives from the Lord "the treasures of darkness, riches stored in secret places" (Isaiah 45:3).

That we might enjoy the blessing of hope, the Spirit works in us, beginning with salvation. Then He uses suffering to increase that hope, and as we suffer, He opens up to us the Word of God. "For everything that was written in the past was written to teach us, so that through endurance and the encouragement of the Scriptures we might have hope" (Romans 15:4). Salvation + suffering + the Scriptures = living hope! "When you pass through the waters,

I will be with you; and when you pass through the rivers, they will not sweep over you. When you walk through the fire, you will not be burned; the flames will not set you ablaze" (Isaiah 43:2).

My wife and I could write a book about the promises the Lord has given us in times of testing. During more than fifty years of marriage and service, whenever we have had to make a major decision or whenever the Lord has permitted us to suffer, we have heard the Father's voice encouraging and guiding us from the Word. Charles Spurgeon said that the promises of God never shone brighter than when read in the furnace of affliction, and we agree with him.

The Holy Spirit not only enables us in the present but also assures us concerning the future. We have the "firstfruits of the Spirit" to guarantee that our body will one day be redeemed and glorified (Romans 8:23). The Sprit has sealed us and marked us to obtain the glorious inheritance God has for us in heaven (Ephesians 1:13–14). The Holy Spirit through the church not only invites sinners to come to Christ today but also prays for the return of Christ (Revelation 22:17). If we are truly living in the Spirit, we will live in the future tense. Three times in the last chapter of the Bible, Jesus announces His return, and our response should be, "Amen. Come, Lord Jesus" (Revelation 22:20).

Here's our benediction translated by Greek scholar Charles B. Williams: "May the hope-inspiring God so fill you with perfect joy and peace through your continuing faith, that you may bubble over with hope by the power of the Holy Spirit."[8]

Let's not settle for less.

CHAPTER 7

THE MYSTERY BENEDICTION

Now to him who is able to establish you by my gospel and the proclamation of Jesus Christ, according to the revelation of the mystery hidden for long ages past, but now revealed and made known through the prophetic writings by the command of the eternal God, so that all nations might believe and obey him—to the only wise God be glory forever through Jesus Christ! Amen (Romans 16:25–27).

THE ENEMY DOESN'T CARE what goes on in local churches as long as our priorities are blurred and our motives are confused. He would rather we were busily occupied with ego-building trivia than with sacrificial service based on biblical essentials. That word *essentials* takes us immediately to Paul's epistle to the Romans, the New Testament book that God has used many times to restore and renew His people. All Scripture is inspired and profitable, but Romans is for many the basic book of Christian doctrine. It gives us the essentials of the faith.

Paul wrote this letter to the believers in Rome in preparation for a long-intended ministry visit among them. Because many untruthful rumors had been spread about Paul and his work, he wanted the assemblies in Rome to know beforehand exactly what he believed and taught. There were both Jews and Gentiles in these churches, and unfortunately this had led to disagreements about the relationship between the Old Testament law and the gospel as well as the place of Israel in God's plan. These matters Paul dealt with in this marvelous epistle, the basic theological treatise for every Christian to study.

The benediction (or doxology) that closes this epistle is unique. For one thing, it is one long sentence consisting of fifty-five words in the original Greek text. But even more, in this benediction Paul summarized many of the spiritual truths he had discussed and defended in the previous chapters. If you compare Romans 1:1–17 with this benediction, you will see that he emphasized the same truths at the beginning of the letter. In this benediction, Paul gives us spiritual priorities every believer and every local church must honor and defend if the church of Jesus Christ is to glorify God and finish His work on earth (John 17:4).

THE MESSAGE OF THE GOSPEL

"MY GOSPEL" AND "the proclamation of Jesus Christ" are the same message, the good news that Jesus the Son of God died and rose again and will save all who repent and call upon Him in faith. God gave this message personally to Paul—which is why he called it "my gospel"—and he devoted his life to declaring the gospel to Jews and Gentiles throughout the Roman world (1 Corinthians 15:1–8). Paul would accept no other gospel than the one God had entrusted to him (Galatians 1). However, he also called this message "our gospel" (2 Corinthians 4:3; 1 Thessalonians 1:5; 2 Thessalonians 2:14), because all true Christians have believed it and will share it with others and, if necessary, will defend it. Without the gospel, there can be no winning of the lost and building of the church.

The righteousness of God as revealed in the gospel is a major theme of the Roman epistle. In the first three chapters, Paul explains the need for righteousness and in chapters 4–5, God's provision for righteousness in Jesus Christ. We are justified by faith and not by religious works. This righteousness is revealed in the everyday lives of believers (chapters 6–8 and 12–16), for justification always leads to sanctification and service. In chapters 9–11, Paul explains God's righteousness in His dealings with Israel.

This message of Christ is the foundation on which we stand as believers and on which local churches must be built. "For no one can lay any foundation other than the one already laid, which is Jesus Christ" (1 Corinthians 3:11). If we are confident of the gospel, then we will be "rooted and built up in [Christ], strengthened in the faith" (Colossians 2:7) and not "blown here and there by every wind of teaching" (Ephesians 4:14).

The gospel not only saves sinners, but it also stabilizes the saints and keeps them true to their Master. Paul was a servant of the gospel as well as a servant of Jesus Christ, for the gospel is the good news about Jesus Christ (Ephesians 3:7; see Colossians 1:23). Paul's message was also Paul's master, and it should be that way in our own lives as well. If we preach grace and practice law, we are disobeying the gospel as well as the Lord. If the gospel is a message of love, then our lives should reveal that love. The gospel speaks of Christ's sacrifice, and so should our lives (Romans 12:1–2). The gospel is for all kinds of sinners; if the local church is an exclusive "religious club" for the elite, we are not mastered by the gospel. To preach the gospel while at the same time using all sorts of deceptive methods is an abomination in God's sight (1 Thessalonians 2:1–12).

Churches need to be established on the gospel because there are people who want to cause divisions and have their own way (Romans 16:17–18), and this is contrary to the gospel. Satan opposes the church (Romans 16:19–20), but loyalty to the gospel will defeat him. How tragic it is when churches abandon preaching the gospel and substitute entertainment, pop psychology lectures, and religious pep talks. *The gospel is the most expensive message ever proclaimed; it cost Jesus Christ His life!* What right do we have to cheapen it?

"There are some, in these apostate days, who think that the church cannot do better than to come down to the world to learn her ways, follow her maxims and acquire her 'culture,'" said

Charles Haddon Spurgeon. "In fact, the notion is that the world is to be conquered by our conformity to it. This is as contrary to Scripture as the light is to the darkness. The more distinct the line between him that feareth God and him that feareth him not, the better all round."[9]

The word *proclamation* in our benediction means, "to declare as the herald of the king." We are under orders as heralds to speak only what the King has told us to speak. To do otherwise is disobedience and treason. We can preach a smooth message and get a big crowd, but getting a crowd is not the same as building the church. "What is highly valued among men is detestable in God's sight" (Luke 16:15).

Our first priority is to glorify Jesus Christ in the preaching and the living of the gospel. The gospel will not only evangelize the lost but also establish the saved.

THE MYSTERY OF THE CHURCH

THE WORD MYSTERY MEANS "a secret hidden by the Lord in times past but now revealed to His church." These "sacred secrets" were unfolded in apostolic days by the Holy Spirit speaking through prophets in the church (Ephesians 2:20; 3:5). Jesus spoke about the mysteries of the kingdom of heaven in Matthew 13, and John mentioned "the mystery of God" in Revelation 10:7. Between these two references you will find Paul writing about the mystery of the olive tree (Romans 11:25), the mystery of Christ and the church (Ephesians 5:32), the mystery of godliness (1 Timothy 3:16), the mystery of the rapture of the church (1 Corinthians 15:51), and the mystery of lawlessness (2 Thessalonians 2:7).

The mystery Paul refers to here is the mystery of Christ. It is a remarkable revelation that believing Jews and Gentiles are "members together of one body, and sharers together in the promise in Christ Jesus" (Ephesians 3:1–6). "There is neither Jew nor Greek, slave nor free, male nor female, for you are all one in Christ Jesus.

If you belong to Christ, then you are Abraham's seed, and heirs according to the promise" (Galatians 3:28–29). After centuries of being separated from the Gentiles, the Jewish people who trusted Christ would now be members of the same spiritual body with the Gentiles. The Jews prided themselves in their rich heritage as the children of Abraham, and some Jews considered the Gentiles to be "dogs." According to them, if Gentiles wanted to be saved, they first had to become Jews. But at the cross, God reversed that and declared that the Jews were lost sinners just like the Gentiles—and then He offered His mercy to both Jews and Gentiles (Romans 3:9–31). The ground is level at the foot of the cross.

That God would save the Gentiles was no mystery in the Old Testament, for God promised Abraham, "All peoples on earth will be blessed through you" (Genesis 12:3; 22:18). The mystery that was revealed especially through Paul was that saved Jews and Gentiles would be united in one body and inherit together the spiritual riches of Christ. It was this message that aroused the opposition of the strict orthodox Jews in the church who wanted to maintain Jewish "superiority" and Old Testament traditions (Acts 6:7; 15:1ff). We call these people "the Judaizers" (see Acts 21:17ff). This issue was discussed and solved at the Jerusalem conference (Acts 15), but the Judaizers continued to hound Paul and create problems in the Gentile congregations (Galatians 1–2; Philippians 3:1–11).

As Christians, we have been "entrusted with the secret things of God" (1 Corinthians 4:1). When we teach the Scriptures, we are like wealthy householders who dispense "new treasures as well as old" (Matthew 13:11–12, 51–52), and we must be able to handle God's Word correctly (2 Timothy 2:15). The Ten Commandments are repeated in the New Testament epistles and applied to the church (with the exception of the fourth, regarding the Sabbath), and the Holy Spirit helps us to obey them (Romans 8:1–4). But we have been delivered from the bondage of the Mosaic law and must not take that burden upon us (Acts 15:1–11; Galatians 5).

To mix old covenant legalism with new covenant grace is to
put the church into bondage, the bondage from which Jesus died
to deliver us. Legalism is subtle. Paul compared it to yeast: just a
small amount gets into the church, and before long it has increased
and infected the whole body (Galatians 5:1–18). Dr. Donald Grey
Barnhouse used to say, "The Book of Hebrews was written to the
Hebrews to tell them to stop being Hebrews"—not ethnically
speaking, of course, but spiritually speaking. Practicing Old Testament law will neither save the sinner nor mature the saint. This is
a priority message and needs to be shared with God's people.

THE Ministry of the Saints

THE MINISTRY OF THE CHURCH is to share the gospel with all nations so that they might obey God, believe in Jesus Christ, and
be saved. Paul gives thanks that the faith of the believers in Rome
was known throughout the Roman world (Romans 1:8; 16:19),
and their witness is a good example for us to follow. Paul himself
worked tirelessly to "call people from among all the Gentiles to the
obedience that comes from faith" (Romans 1:5).

During my years of itinerant ministry, I often preached in
church sanctuaries that had this sign over the entrance: *ENTER
TO WORSHIP—DEPART TO SERVE.* We call our Sunday meetings "services," but the service really begins when we leave the
church premises and enter the workplace and the neighborhood.
"Those who had been scattered preached the word wherever they
went" (Acts 8:4). The word translated "preached" is simply *evan-
gelized.* They seized every opportunity God gave them and shared
the good news about Jesus Christ.

God doesn't suggest that perhaps we consider telling people
about Jesus. He commands it. Paul's words are "by command of
the eternal God." As the finance committee prepares the annual
church budget, the big question is not "What can we afford to do?"
but "What does the Lord command us to do?" *And He is able to*

accomplish His will in us and through us. Paul opened this benediction by affirming the sovereign power of God: "He is able!" God's ability and our availability can together do great things. When you consider the marvelous means of communication and transportation we have today, surely we can do a better job of giving the gospel to the world. Paul called the Lord "the only wise God." He is a God of wisdom and power. He knows what He wants to do, and He is able to get it done. But He has limited Himself to use us as His tools, and we must be yielded to Him.

During my teen years, I heard many preachers who challenged listeners to give their lives to Christ for full-time service, but that challenge is rarely heard today. Why? Godly parents used to pray that the Lord would call their children into His service. I know that not every believer is called to serve Christ in some type of vocational ministry and that full-time Christian living must take priority in our lives, regardless of our vocation. But surely the harvest is still plentiful and the laborers are few, and if the situation is to change, churches need both to pray for laborers and seek to enlist them.

The Motive of God's Glory

WHAT A MAGNIFICENT WAY to end this benediction: ". . . to the only wise God be glory forever through Jesus Christ! Amen." God's people need to be reminded that what we do is not for our praise but for the glory of God. If we have any other motive, God will not bless our service. The Son glorifies the Father (John 17:1), and the Holy Spirit glorifies the Son (John 16:14). If we sincerely seek to glorify Christ, the Holy Spirit will give us the power to work and witness (Acts 1:8), and the Son and the Father will be glorified. If we seek our own glory, nothing much will happen, and what does happen won't last.

At least twenty-one times in this letter, Paul mentions *glory* in one way or another. The sinful world exchanged the glory of the living God for dead idols (Romans 1:23), and lost sinners are still following that bad example and falling short of God's glory (Romans 3:23). The lost world has no hope of glory, but Christians "rejoice in the hope of the glory of God" (Romans 5:2). No matter what we may suffer today, it is "not worth comparing with the glory that will be revealed in us" (Romans 8:18). In fact, all creation is awaiting the coming of Christ, when creation will be delivered from "bondage to decay and brought into the glorious freedom of the children of God" (Romans 8:21).

"And those he predestined, he also called; those he called, he also justified; those he justified, he also glorified" (Romans 8:30). Note the tense of that verb—*glorified*. The Greek tense means that it has already happened, even though we may not look like it. "I have given them the glory that you gave me," Jesus said to His Father (John 17:22). We have it now! All that has to happen is for Jesus to return, and His glory will be revealed.

Why, then, live to glorify ourselves? "All men [people] are like grass, and all their glory is like the flowers of the field," wrote Isaiah. "The grass withers and the flowers fall, but the word of our God stands forever" (Isaiah 40:6, 8). "For from him and through him and to him are all things. To him be the glory forever! Amen" (Romans 11:36).

Can you sincerely say amen to that?

CHAPTER 8

THE BENEDICTION OF POWER

Now to him who is able to do immeasurably more than all we ask or imagine, according to his power that is at work within us, to him be glory in the church and in Christ Jesus throughout all generations, forever and ever! Amen (Ephesians 3:20–21).

I T ALL STARTED WITH muscle power, and then horsepower got into the picture, followed by waterpower. The invention of gunpowder and TNT brought in a destructive power unknown before. Steam power helped to usher in the Industrial Revolution, and electric power moved things along even faster. Now we're in the era of atomic power, which can either serve the world or destroy it. Go to the stock exchange and you find financial power, to the university and you see the power of knowledge. We live in a world that focuses on power.

This benediction focuses on three aspects of divine power.

ABILITY

FOR CHRISTIAN BELIEVERS, the most awesome power in the universe is the power of God. He is God Almighty, the omnipotent one. Job had it right: "I know that you can do all things; no plan of yours can be thwarted" (42:2). "Is anything too hard for the Lord?" God asked both Abraham (Genesis 18:14) and the prophet Jeremiah (Jeremiah 32:27; see 32:17). "With man this is impossible," said Jesus, "but with God all things are possible" (Matthew 19:26; see Mark 10:27).

Most people don't like to admit that they are weak and unable to accomplish all they dream about or talk about. Political candidates make promises they can never fulfill, not because they don't want to but because they aren't able to. Their intentions are excellent, but their resources are poor. Jesus warned His disciples, "Apart from me, you can do nothing" (John 15:5). The apostle Paul wrote, "For when I am weak, then I am strong" (2 Corinthians 11:10). His secret? "I can do everything through him who gives me strength" (Philippians 4:13).

Paul coined a new word, *huperekperissou,* which means "superabundantly beyond." The Greek *huper* becomes our English prefix *hyper; ek* means "out of"; and *perissou* means "the overflow, the abundance." It all becomes "over and above the overflow."

When the Jews wanted to give an example of the greatness of God's power, they pointed back to the opening of the Red Sea and Israel's exodus from Egypt. But Paul had a picture far greater than that: the resurrection of Jesus Christ from the dead. Paul prayed that the saints might experience "his incomparably great power for us who believe. That power is like the working of his mighty strength, which he exerted in Christ when he raised him from the dead and seated him at his right hand in the heavenly realms" (Ephesians 1:19–20). He prayed that God would "strengthen [them] with power through his Spirit in [their] inner being . . . that [they] may be filled to the measure of all the fullness of God" (Ephesians 3:16, 19). He told the church in Philippi, "I want to know Christ and the power of his resurrection . . ." (Philippians 3:10), and that should also be our goal in life.

What is God able to do? Among other things, He is able to

- deliver His servants from trouble (Daniel 3:17)
- keep all His promises (Romans 4:20–21)
- keep His servants standing (Romans 14:4)
- establish His people (Romans 16:25)

- provide escape from temptation (1 Corinthians 10:13–14)
- make all grace abound to His people (2 Corinthians 9:8)
- guard His own to the end (2 Timothy 1:12)
- help those who come to Him (Hebrews 2:18)
- save his people completely (Hebrews 7:25)
- keep the saints from falling (Jude 24)

The mistake we make is thinking that God's mighty wonders were possible centuries ago, but they are impossible today. We're like Gideon who asked the angel, "But, sir, if the Lord is with us, why has all this [trouble] happened to us? Where are all his wonders that our fathers told us about?" (Judges 6:13). But the angel already called Gideon "a mighty warrior" (Judges 6:12), and that was all the encouragement he needed to step out by faith and defeat the enemy. If God says you are a "mighty warrior," then you are! So act like it and trust His power.

If we think that God's mighty power is available only for apostolic miracles, we are wrong. God's power is available today to provide strength in difficult circumstances, such as when our physician prescribes surgery or diagnoses cancer. When we're stuck in a traffic jam or when the children start getting on our nerves, we can draw upon the power of the Lord, for "with God all things are possible" (Matthew 19:26). He is "able to do immeasurably more."

One more important fact: note that the Lord enables us *according to* his power" and not "*out of* his power." If a billionaire gives me five dollars, it comes "out of" his wealth and is really not a generous gift. But if he gives me a million dollars, that is "according to" his wealth. God is not bankrupt and never gives as though He were. John Newton's hymn "Come, My Soul, Thy Suit Prepare" says it beautifully:

Thou art coming to a King,
Large petitions with thee bring;

For His grace and power are such,
None can ever ask too much.

AVAILABILITY

GOD IS ABLE, but He's made it possible for us to be able to work with Him to get things done. When we were born, the Lord supervised the creation of our genetic structure so that we would have certain abilities (Psalm 139:13–16). When we were born again, the Holy Spirit gave us gifts to match our abilities. All of God's children have what they need for successful, dedicated service and are constantly being equipped as they grow in grace and knowledge (Hebrews 13:20–21; 2 Peter 3:18).

The key phrase in this benediction is "the power that is at work in us." Where is His power? In us. How does that power work? Through us. What a remarkable thing that our great God should give us His Holy Spirit to dwell in us and to work in and through us, "for it is God who works in you to will and to act according to his good purpose" (Philippians 2:13). The verb translated "works" gives us the English word *energy*. The devil is at work energizing unbelievers (Ephesians 2:2), but the resurrection power of God is at work in believers energizing them for ministry (Ephesians 1:19–20). This is how God "works out" His purposes in this world (Ephesians 1:11). Yes, He could send legions of angels, but He deigns to use His own children to accomplish His purposes in this world. The main thing is that we are available to Him "in season and out of season."

"There are four kinds of people in the church," one of my seminary professors used to remind us. "There are those who *make* things happen, those who *watch* things happen, those who *criticize* what's happening, and those who *don't know anything's happening.*" In other words, the four kinds of people are the workers, the spectators, the complainers, and the clueless. The thing that made Moses a leader was that he not only knew *what* God was doing but also *why* He was doing it (Psalm 103:7). Like Moses, we must be available to the Lord for the three important ministries Paul points out in our benediction: praying, planning, and participating—asking, thinking, doing.

First, we must pray so that we will know God's will. Moses and Paul were men of prayer, and so were Samuel, David, Ezra, and Nehemiah, the prophets and the apostles. And thank God for the women who could pray—Deborah, Hannah, Esther, Mary the mother of Jesus, Elizabeth her kinswoman, the mother of John Mark, and many more. We don't pray only in emergencies but "continually" (1 Thessalonians 5:17), always seeking to know His will for us. God's will comes from God's heart (Psalm 33:11), and like John, we must be close to His heart so we can love Him and listen to Him (John 13:23; 21:20).

Sometimes the Lord gives us every detail of what we're supposed to do. He did this for Noah in the building of the ark, Moses in the construction of the tabernacle, Joshua in the conquest of Jericho, Solomon in the building of the temple, and Paul when he sent him to minister in Philippi. It's encouraging when God guides us in such a detailed way, but that isn't always how he works. There are times when we have to make plans and start moving and trust God to open and close doors. Before Paul got the command to go to Philippi, he tried to go to Asia and then to Bithynia, but the doors were closed (Acts 16:6–10); at least he kept moving and seeking God's will. Have you ever tried to steer an automobile and make progress when the gear is in park?

We keep praying as we make our plans, and we make those plans according to the promises and principles clearly stated in the Bible. Like the apostles, we make prayer and the Word our daily priorities (Acts 6:4). This is where planning comes in. The Lord expects us to use our minds in determining what He wants us to do. This doesn't mean we depend on our own understanding (Proverbs 3:5–6) but that we use our minds to understand the

Word, assess the circumstances, and make some Spirit-led decisions that will honor the Lord. Sometimes this isn't easy, but it has to be done. We decide and then we start to take steps, and if our path is the wrong one, the Lord will slam the doors—unless we stubbornly want our own way. How many times I have been grateful for Philippians 3:15—"And if on some point you think differently, that too God will make clear to you." The important thing is that we cultivate a sensitive spirit, an open mind, and a surrendered will. John 7:17 is also a great encouragement: "Anyone who wants to do the will of God will know" (NLT).

As we plan, we trust God to enlighten and guide us. "There is no wisdom, no insight, no plan that can succeed against the Lord" (Proverbs 21:30). "Commit to the Lord whatever you do, and your plans will succeed" (Proverbs 16:3). "In their hearts human beings plan their course, but the Lord establishes their steps" (Proverbs 16:9 TNIV). "Many are the plans in a human heart, but it is the Lord's purpose that prevails" (Proverbs 19:21 TNIV). But we also take advantage of the wisdom and experience of others, always testing it by the Word of God. "The plans of the righteous are just, but the advice of the wicked is deceitful" (Proverbs 12:5). "Make plans by seeking advice; if you wage war, obtain guidance" (Proverbs 20:18). Finally, we must be patient and wait on the Lord for His providential guidance. "The plans of the diligent lead to profit as surely as haste leads to poverty" (Proverbs 21:5). One of the evidences that we are acting by faith is that we cultivate patience, for it is through faith and patience that we inherit what God has promised (Hebrews 6:12).

We pray, we plan, and we participate. We are not here just to seek God's will and give good advice. We are here to do God's will and accomplish His purposes in the world. The first place God answers prayer is often in the life of the one praying. Moses in Midian was praying for his people enslaved in Egypt, and God called Moses to deliver them. Nehemiah was praying about the plight of the Jews in Jerusalem, and God called him to go there and rebuild the walls. Queen Esther was distressed because the king had ordered her people destroyed. She prayed, and God sent her to intercede with the king. Prayer must never be a substitute for action, for "faith by itself, if it is not accompanied by action, is dead" (James 2:17).

If we are serious when we pray for God's will to be done and His work accomplished, then we should be available to be a part of the answer. Luke 9:57–10:2 reports how Jesus called two men to follow Him, but they both had excuses and said no. A third man volunteered if Jesus would accept his conditions, but the man backed out. None of these potential world-changers was willing to pay the price to follow Jesus. "The harvest is plentiful, but the workers are few," said the Lord to His disciples. After reading about the three would-be followers, are we surprised that the workers are few? Then what's the solution to the problem? "Ask the Lord of the harvest, therefore, to send out workers into his harvest field." The answer is prayer. Those who sincerely pray usually end up laboring in the harvest.

The Lord is still seeking laborers (Ezekiel 22:30; Isaiah 59:15–16).

Responsibility

WHY DOES THE LORD SHARE His ability with us? Why do we make ourselves and our abilities and gifts available to Him? *For the eternal glory of the Lord Jesus Christ!* Paul concludes the benediction with "to him be glory in the church and in Christ Jesus throughout all generations, for ever and ever! Amen."

The ultimate purpose of the plan of salvation is "to the praise of His glory" (Ephesians 1:6, 12, 14). Jesus didn't die to solve our problems; He died to glorify the Father (John 12:27–28). The Father has a glorious inheritance in the saints (Ephesians 1:18) that will not be fully revealed until Jesus returns and the church is glorified in heaven. We have God's glory now, dwelling within us in the person of the Holy Spirit (John 17:22), and one day we shall see Christ's glory in heaven (John 17:5, 22). But the church will also glorify the Father and the Son forever. What a future!

What the church is, says, and does in the world today should always glorify the Father and the Son. The first request in the Lord's Prayer is "Hallowed be your name" (Matthew 6:9), so our praying must glorify Him. Our good works must honor God's name and not our own (Matthew 5:16). Even our sufferings for Christ will one day be turned into glory (Romans 8:18; 1 Peter 4:12–19). We should even glorify the Lord in our death (John 21:19; Philippians 1:20–21). When Jesus appears, we shall appear with Him in glory (Colossians 3:4). We shall see His glory and share His glory for eternity.

But the glory Paul wrote about in Ephesians 3:21 is the glory the church will bring to the Father and the Son *throughout eternity in heaven*. The more we glorify the Lord here on earth, the more we will glorify Him with all believers in heaven. Today, the church has stains and wrinkles and blemishes, but one day Jesus will present His church to the Father "as a radiant church" without one defect (Ephesians 5:25–27). We shall worship the Lord "resplendent in His glory," and what a worship time that will be! In this life, we are sometimes ashamed of ourselves and of the church, but "we know that when he appears, we shall be like him, for we shall see him as he is" (1 John 3:2).

Our motive for Christian living and service is not to impress people or even gain rewards, but to glorify the Father and the Son in the power of the Holy Spirit. This is how the Bride makes herself ready for the glorious wedding and marriage feast in heaven (Revelation 19:6–8). In this life, we Christians are prone to think of individual service, or perhaps the service of individual churches and parachurch ministries, but one day all of this will be put together into one magnificent display of God's glory.

Someone has said that *responsibility* means "our response to God's ability," and I agree. As we read the Word, we discover what His ability really is. As we make ourselves available to Him, we share in that ability as He works in us and through us. No matter how heavy the burdens or pressing the battles, one day we will "exchange our cross for a crown" and share the eternal glory of God.

Why not begin today?

CHAPTER 9

THE BENEDICTION OF LOVE

Peace to the brothers, and love with faith from God the Father and the Lord Jesus Christ. Grace to all who love our Lord Jesus Christ with an undying love (Ephesians 6:23–24).

THE APOSTLE PAUL was not ashamed to ask his friends to pray for him (Ephesians 6:19–20), nor was he remiss in praying for them. Whenever he mentioned his friends at the throne of grace, Paul was loving them "at a distance," and God recognized this love and honored his faith.

But Paul didn't end the Ephesian letter with an emphasis on prayer, as important as that is. He ended the letter with an emphasis on love. Christian love is an act of the will; it means treating others the way the Lord treats us. Christian love isn't a fuzzy feeling that we piously work up; it's a precious fruit that the Holy Spirit produces in our hearts as we walk in the will of God. "But the fruit of the Spirit is love" (Galatians 5:22). "God has poured out his love into our hearts by the Holy Spirit, whom he has given us" (Romans 5:5). Love is an important theme in the Ephesian epistle and is mentioned at least thirteen times.

In this benediction, Paul mentions three recipients of Christian love whom we must not ignore.

OUR BELOVED CO-WORKERS (EPHESIANS 6:21–22)

TYCHICUS WAS AN IMPORTANT member of Paul's missionary team. Paul called him "the dear brother and faithful servant in the Lord" (Ephesians 6:21) and "a dear brother, a faithful minister and fellow servant in the Lord" (Colossians 4:7).

He was probably from Ephesus (see Acts 20:4) and was the kind of believer Paul could send anywhere and know that he would accomplish the assignment. He accompanied Paul through Macedonia and Greece (Acts 20:1–6), replaced Timothy in Ephesus (2 Timothy 4:12), and followed Titus in Crete (Titus 3:12). When he carried this epistle to the church in Ephesus, he also carried a letter to the believers in Colosse and a personal letter from Paul to Philemon in Colosse (Colossians 4:7–9). Thanks to the providence of God and the faithfulness of Tychicus, we have these letters today and can study them for our personal edification.

As you read the book of Acts and the epistles of Paul, you can't help but notice Paul's dependence on his co-workers and his appreciation for them. At least thirty-six different men and women are named as fellow workers with Paul, and there were many more whose names were never included. Tychicus is mentioned five times, and Paul made it clear that his co-worker was a beloved and faithful servant of Jesus Christ. Paul didn't issue orders to his associates the way a general commands his officers, because their first responsibility was to the Lord. Rather, he prayed for them, shared his plans, and helped them to find God's will. Paul's saying, "I hope in the Lord Jesus to send Timothy to you soon" (Philippians 2:19) suggests that he was a spiritual director rather than an organizational dictator. Titus 3:13 makes it clear that these many friends not only helped Paul but also helped one another. Paul believed in networking, and the Lord used those contacts to strengthen and expand the outreach of the church.

Let's not be guilty of taking our fellow workers for granted. "Carry each other's burdens, and in this way you will fulfill the law of Christ" (Galatians 6:2). There are more people involved in the Lord's service than those who stand in the spotlight, on the platform, or before the television cameras. Preachers, teachers, and musicians get the credit for building the church, but they know how limited they would be without a host of unnamed people who serve behind the scenes. This includes the men and women who care for the building and manage the equipment, the people working in the kitchen, the office staff, the people who manage the parking facilities in all kinds of weather, greeters and ushers, and many more.

Paul trusted Tychicus to tell the congregations in Ephesus and Colosse the truth about his situation in Rome. Paul could have closed his letter by dictating an autobiographical paragraph, but instead he left it to Tychicus to share the facts, knowing that he would tell the truth. He also knew that Tychicus would share the news in such a way that the believers would be encouraged. There is no substitute for a trustworthy messenger (Proverbs 25:13).

Tychicus ministered with Paul in all kinds of circumstances and officially represented him to the churches to which he was sent. Paul was a Roman prisoner, but Tychicus was free to move about and minister to the congregations, most of which Paul had founded. What a help he was to Paul will only be known when God's people are gathered together in heaven. Meanwhile, in his service he's a good example for us to follow, and Paul in his gratitude is also worth imitating.

Our Beloved Church Congregations (Ephesians 6:22–23)

PAUL HAD MINISTERED in Ephesus for nearly three years (Acts 19:8–10; 20–31) and, during that time, had seen many come to Christ and be built up in the faith. One of those new believers, Epaphras, had taken the message from Ephesus to Colosse, where he founded a church (Colossians 1:7; 4:12–13). A true pastor, Paul's heart was bound to the hearts of his people, and their hearts were bound to him. They loved him and wanted to know how things were going in Rome, where Paul was under house arrest. They knew that Paul prayed for them, and they in turn prayed for Paul, and they wanted their praying to be intelligent and on target.

It's tragic when the love of local churches grows cold toward God's servants, whether toward the pastors God sends them, former pastors, or the missionaries the church sends out to reach others. Paul named in verse 23 the three essentials for a vibrant church: peace, love, and faith. In his greeting at the beginning of the letter, Paul invoked the blessings of God's grace and peace (Ephesians 1:2). In the middle of the letter, he urged them to maintain "the unity of the Spirit through the bond of peace" (Ephesians 4:3), and at the close of the letter, he again emphasized peace (Ephesians 6:15). The grace of God leads us to faith in Jesus Christ, faith ought to produce love for one another (Ephesians 1:15), and love should produce peace (see Romans 5:1–5). These are the "living links" that bind the saints together.

Everything wasn't perfect in the Ephesian church, nor is any church perfect, because churches are made up of people, and people aren't perfect. The saints at Ephesus were not taking advantage of their spiritual privileges, so Paul prayed that their eyes would be opened to the power and wealth available to them in Christ (Ephesians 1:15ff; 3:14ff). There was some disunity in the body because the believers were impatient with each other and failed to manifest love (Ephesians 4:1ff). Some of them were living outright worldly lives, acting and speaking like lost sinners and not like God's children (Ephesians 4:17ff). Some of the marriages and families were marked by rebellion and disobedience instead of love and submission (Ephesians 5:22ff). The members of the church in Ephesus were certainly not living like those who were seated with Christ in the heavenlies (Ephesians 2:6).

But Paul didn't give up on them. He reminded them of their privileged position in Christ and urged them to be filled with the Spirit and not to imitate the world. He warned them against the wiles of the devil and commanded them to put on the whole armor of God. He sent Tychicus to deliver the Ephesian epistle and also to update them on his situation in Rome. Blessed are those believers in the local churches who want to know what is going on in the lives of God's servants and who are faithful to pray for them and help them.

It's discouraging to see how few churches today can conduct a successful missionary conference. I once heard a church officer say to the pastor, "I don't care how much money or prayer you want for our missionaries, just don't make me listen to them!" Missionaries come home from the field wanting to share blessings and burdens, and only a remnant of the church congregation comes to hear their reports. Imagine serving for years on a difficult field only to visit your home church and be given eight minutes in the Sunday service for your report.

Our Beloved Savior and Lord (6:24)

When Jesus restored Peter to discipleship and service, three times He asked him, "Do you love me?" (John 21:15–17). Why? Because loving Jesus Christ is essential for successful Christian ministry. Jesus didn't ask Peter about doctrine or methodology, as important as they are. Rather, He focused on the heart—Peter's love for Jesus Christ. Yes, it's important that we love the lost and love one another, but both of those are the results of our loving Jesus Christ "with an undying love."

The word translated "undying" in Ephesians 6:24 is translated "imperishable" in 1 Corinthians 15:42, 50 and 53–54, referring to the glorious resurrection body of the believer. "Undying love" is love made deeper and stronger in the experiences of life. It's love that is sincere and devoted, love that comes from a heart that is not divided. "If anyone does not love the Lord—a curse be on him," wrote Paul (1 Corinthians 16:22). That sounds serious!

True believers experience the love of God in their hearts because God's Spirit is present there and at work (Romans 5:5). Our love for Christ motivates us to hear His Word and obey it. "If you love me, you will obey what I command" (John 14:15). To obey out of fear or because we want to "earn" some blessing is to miss the point completely. "Whom have I in heaven but you? And earth has nothing I desire besides you." That's how Asaph described his love for the Lord in Psalm 73:25. Nothing could replace it.

It was in their love for Jesus that the church at Ephesus eventually failed. "Yet I hold this against you: You have forsaken your first love" (Revelation 2:4). The believers in Ephesus worked hard to maintain the purity of the church and to advance the work God had given them, but slowly their love began to grow cold. The "machinery" of the church was still operating, but the fire had died down in their hearts. They were no longer serving in love. "First love" is love that characterizes a husband and wife in their early days of marriage and matures as the years go by (Jeremiah 2:1–2). It isn't the shallow excitement of "romance"—being "in love with love"—but the deepening enrichment of a love that leads to sacrifice and service, forgiveness and faithfulness, and that follows the pattern given in 1 Corinthians 13.

When in Christian love we sacrifice so we can serve others, and we do it for the sake of Jesus Christ, we are loving the Lord Jesus (Matthew 25:31–46). The reward of loving is found in cultivating a heart like the Master's and entering into a fellowship with Him that nothing in this world can give or even rival. It's relatively easy to sing or speak about our love for the Lord, but to prove it by our actions is quite another thing.

Grace, peace, and faith bind together the hearts of believers who love Jesus Christ with an undying love. People who truly love Christ will love one another and give all the glory to the Lord. Their worship and service will exalt the Lord, and not the pastor or the church. Undying love for Christ leads to unchanging love for one another, unwavering faith in the promises of God, unfailing grace to meet every need, and unbelievable peace among the children of God. The heart of every problem is the problem in the heart, and heart problems are solved by sincere love for Jesus.

CHAPTER 10

THE GRACE BENEDICTIONS

The grace of our Lord Jesus Christ be with you (1 Thessalonians 5:28).

I, Paul, write this greeting in my own hand, which is the distinguishing mark in all my letters. This is how I write. The grace of our Lord Jesus Christ be with you all (2 Thessalonians 3:17–18).

THE SALUTATIONS AND BENEDICTIONS in Paul's letters focus on the grace of God. In each letter, Paul's salutation first identifies the writer or writers, then names the recipients, and then concludes with "Grace and peace to you from God our Father and the Lord Jesus Christ." The thirteen benedictions follow a similar pattern: "The grace of our Lord Jesus Christ be with you." Paul uses the word *grace* more than one hundred times in Acts and his thirteen epistles. *Grace* was obviously one of the key words in Paul's theological vocabulary. Everything that we are, have, and do that pleases and honors the Lord is the result of His grace in our lives.

The inspired contents of each epistle are "wrapped up" in grace from the beginning to end. Grace is the alpha, and grace is the omega. As we begin to read an epistle, grace encourages us to keep on reading, and when we get to the end, grace encourages us to remember what we have learned and obey it. The fact that we even possess these letters and can read them is because of God's grace. What Paul said of himself, we must say of ourselves: "But by the grace of God I am what I am" (1 Corinthians 15:10).

Sometimes grace stands alone in the text, and other times it is linked with another Christian virtue and blessing.

GRACE AND TRUTH

IT WAS THE APOSTLE John who joined these two and then illustrated them in his gospel. Jesus Christ is "full of grace and truth" (John 1:14), and, "Grace and truth came through Jesus Christ" (John 1:17). They go together. Truth reveals the need, and grace meets the need, as we trust Jesus Christ.

At the wedding feast in Cana, the truth was that there was no wine, but grace stepped in and met the need. The truth was that Nicodemus, with all his religion, was a lost sinner, but Jesus in His grace offered him new birth. The Samaritan woman at the well tried to avoid admitting the truth that she was a much-married failure who was now living with a man not her husband. When she admitted it, then she was a candidate for the grace that saved her. She not only believed in Jesus but also encouraged the people in her city to believe in Him. In John's gospel, whether you look at the invalid at the pool, the hungry multitude, the woman caught in adultery, or the blind beggar, you see grace and truth in operation (chapters 5–9). Truth reveals the need, and grace supplies the need.

As an unconverted Pharisee, Paul knew that "the law was given through Moses," but he wasn't saved until he realized that "grace and truth came through Jesus Christ" (John 1:17) and trusted Jesus to save him. If we reject God's truth, we have no access to God's grace, but if we accept God's truth, the grace of God is available to meet our needs as we trust Jesus. Like the wine at the wedding feast in Cana, the Jewish religion had run out and had nothing to offer. It was like that row of empty jars waiting to be filled (John 2:6).

Paul's "Grace" Salutations and Benedictions

Romans 1:7 and 16:20	1 Thessalonians 1:1 and 5:28
1 Corinthians 1:3 and 16:23	2 Thessalonians 1:2 and 3:18
2 Corinthians 1:2 and 13:14	1 Timothy 1:2 and 6:21
Galatians 1:3 and 6:18	2 Timothy 1:2 and 4:22
Ephesians 1:2 and 6:24	Titus 1:4 and 3:15
Philippians 1:2 and 4:23	Philemon 3 and 25
Colossians 1:2 and 4:18	

Paul chose to make *grace* his personal apostolic identification mark. "I, Paul, write this greeting in my own hand, which is the distinguishing mark in all my letters. This is how I write. The grace of our Lord Jesus Christ be with you all" (2 Thessalonians 3:17–18). Paul dictated his letters to a secretary (Romans 16:22) and then added his own signature and "grace mark" at the end (1 Corinthians 16:21; Galatians 6:11; Colossians 4:18). This was necessary because the enemy was circulating forged letters that were teaching false doctrines (2 Thessalonians 2:1–2). Satan is a counterfeiter, and, just as in Paul's day, today false "gospels" and "epistles" are available in most bookstores and many pulpits and even on movie theater screens (Galatians 1:1–10). Human nature is such that people find it easy to believe lies but difficult to face the truth.

GRACE AND PEACE

As WE HAVE SEEN, this was Paul's standard greeting in his letters. It was a combination of the ancient Jewish greeting *shalom-peace* and the Christian greeting *grace*. Peter also used this greeting (1 Peter 1:2; 2 Peter 1:2), as did John (Revelation 1:4), and Paul used it as a benediction in 2 Thessalonians 3:16. We will study this benediction later in this book.

Suffice it to say here that the one thing the world is seeking— peace—is available only in the one way the world won't accept—

grace. Grace implies that sinners are bankrupt. There is nothing they can give or do that will provide the peace of mind or peace of heart that only Jesus can provide.

GRACE, MERCY, AND PEACE

PAUL USED THIS GREETING in 1 Timothy 1:2 and 2 Timothy 1:2, but nowhere else in his epistles. He had appointed Timothy to replace him in Ephesus, and Paul's two letters reveal that his young successor was facing some difficulties. To begin with, it wouldn't be easy to follow a great leader like Paul. The city itself was steeped in idolatry, and to take a stand for Jesus Christ meant paying a price. False teachers had invaded the fellowship, and there were problems within the church's leadership that were affecting the public worship. There are hints of divisions between the generations, and Timothy also had physical problems that made it difficult to do his work. Ulcers, perhaps?

Those who are called to minister the Word and shepherd the flock need both the grace and mercy of the Lord, because we have nothing in ourselves that can make us faithful ministers of Jesus Christ. All we can do is depend on the grace and mercy of the Lord. "And who is equal to such a task?" asked Paul (2 Corinthians 2:16). His answer: "Not that we are competent in ourselves to claim anything for ourselves, but our competence comes from God" (2 Corinthians 3:5). God in His grace gives us what we don't deserve, and in His mercy He doesn't give us what we do deserve. "Therefore, since through God's mercy we have this ministry, we do not lose heart" (2 Corinthians 4:1).

GRACE AND GLORY

"FOR THE LORD GOD is a sun and shield; the Lord gives grace and glory" (Psalm 84:11 NASB). Whatever begins with God's grace will end up revealing God's glory. As the Old Testament high priest approached the tabernacle, he came first to the altar where the sacrifices were offered to the Lord. That was the grace of God, the innocent animal shedding its blood for the guilty sinner. But beyond the veil at the other end of the tabernacle stood the Holy of Holies where the glory of God was enthroned between the cherubim. From grace to glory! By faith we come to the cross where Jesus shed His blood making our redemption possible, and this gracious redemption leads ultimately to the glory of God (Ephesians 1:7, 12, 14).

God gives His grace to those who want to glorify Him. As we suffer for the Lord, we may not experience that glory today, but we can be sure that God will ultimately be glorified. "I consider that our present sufferings are not worth comparing with the glory that will be revealed in us" (Romans 8:18). "For our light and momentary troubles are achieving for us an eternal glory that far outweighs them all" (2 Corinthians 4:17). "But rejoice that you participate in the sufferings of Christ, so that you may be overjoyed when his glory is revealed" (1 Peter 4:13).

Is it any wonder that Paul emphasized the grace of God so much in his letters? He had experienced that grace and been born into the family of God. During his years of ministry, he had received one blessing of grace after another (John 1:16), and he had seen the grace of God work in the lives of many people. Grace was the message on his lips and the motivation in his heart. It was also the "mark" of authenticity on his letters.

CHAPTER 11

THE HEART BENEDICTIONS

May the Lord make your love increase and overflow for each other and for everyone else, just as ours does for you. May he strengthen your hearts so that you will be blameless and holy in the presence of our God and Father when our Lord Jesus comes with all his holy ones (1 Thessalonians 3:12–13).

May the Lord direct your hearts into God's love and Christ's perseverance (2 Thessalonians 3:5).

SOME BIBLE STUDENTS like to call these brief requests "wish prayers" and not benedictions, but what we call them doesn't alter their character, and surely they may be used as benedictions. There are more of these brief prayers in the Thessalonian correspondence than in any of the other letters Paul wrote (1 Thessalonians 3:11; 3:12–13; 5:23; 5:28; 2 Thessalonians 1:11–12; 2:16–17; 3:5; 3:16; 3:18). The Thessalonian believers were young in the faith and were experiencing severe persecution at the hands of the enemies of the gospel, and Paul's prayers helped them to keep going victoriously for the Lord.

But Satan not only opposed them as the devouring lion (1 Peter 5:8–9) but also as the deceiving serpent (2 Corinthians 11:1–4). Somebody had sent the church a forged letter as if from Paul, stating that the tribulation was now taking place (2 Thessalonians 2:1–12), and this upset the saints considerably. There may also have been a counterfeit "word of prophecy" given in a public meeting. "Test everything" was Paul's admonition to them. Not everything spoken in public church meetings is necessarily the Word of God (1 Thessalonians 5:20–22).

The emphasis in these benedictions is on the condition of the believer's heart. "Above all else, guard your heart, for it is the wellspring of life" (Proverbs 4:23). An unguarded heart soon becomes an undisciplined and unspiritual heart, and the consequences are disastrous. Paul commanded Christian slaves to do the will of God from their hearts (Ephesians 6:6), but that command applies to all believers. Jonah finally ended up doing the will of God, but it wasn't from his heart, so his obedience brought him no blessing (Jonah 4).

These benedictions describe the characteristics of the heart God wants for each of His children.

A SURRENDERED HEART

"MAY THE LORD DIRECT your hearts" (2 Thessalonians 3:5) implies that the Thessalonians had yielded their hearts to the Lord and desired His guidance in every decision they would make and every step they would take. David's prayer after the great offering for the temple focuses on this essential: "O Lord, God of our fathers Abraham, Isaac and Israel, keep this desire [to give generously] in the hearts of your people forever, and keep their hearts loyal to you" (1 Chronicles 29:18). If we have loving hearts, we will have loyal hearts and obey the will of God no matter how we feel or what the consequences might be. "Not my will, but yours be done" (Luke 22:42) is the key to a surrendered heart and a guided life.

"Things seen are of little real significance in the light of God's presence," wrote A. W. Tozer in *The Next Chapter After the Last*. "He pays small attention to the beauty of a woman or the strength of a man. With Him the heart is all that matters" (p. 82). Proverbs 4:23 calls the heart "the wellspring of life," and that says it all. When God directs the heart, He never takes us on detours.

A Loving Heart

WE SURRENDER OUR HEARTS because we love Him, and the Lord answers by directing our hearts into a greater and deeper experience of His love. "If anyone loves me," said Jesus, "he will obey my teaching. My Father will love him, and we will come to him and make our home with him" (John 14:23). Paul had this truth in mind when he prayed for the Ephesian believers that "Christ may dwell in your hearts through faith" (Ephesians 3:17), for the word *dwell* means "to settle down and feel at home." Does Jesus feel at home in our hearts and want to love us even more? Just as parents want to love their children in deeper ways and want their children to love them, so our Father and our Savior want to share their love with us in deeper ways. Only those who are willing to pay the price of surrender enjoy the experience of this deeper love.

Some believers are afraid of what they call emotional experiences, but the Lord made our emotions and wants to satisfy them in His way. Yes, feelings can lead us astray, but not if we are yielded to the Lord, waiting on Him, and following His Word. Paul's prayer in 1 Thessalonians 3:12 proves the Lord's desire that our love increase. He wants the love in our hearts to "increase and overflow," not only for the Lord and for other believers, but also "for everyone else." That includes a great many people! As the leader, Paul set the example for this love, because the sheep aren't likely to go beyond the example of the shepherd. See 1 Thessalonians 2:8–11 and 3:12.

God's children have been "taught by God to love each other" (1 Thessalonians 4:9). The Father teaches us to love because He first loved us and sent His Son to save us (1 John 4:19). Jesus teaches us to love, for He commanded His followers to love one another and proved His love by dying on the cross (John 13:34; 15:13). The Holy Spirit teaches us to love one another by filling our surrendered hearts with depths of His love (Romans 5:5). If God's children don't love one another, it's because they don't love the Lord, and not to love the Lord is a serious sin. "If anyone does not love the Lord—a curse be on him" (1 Corinthians 16:22). As a noun or a verb, the word *love* is found at least a dozen times in the two Thessalonian epistles. Paul considered it important, and so should we.

A STEADFAST HEART

THE PHRASE "CHRIST'S PERSEVERANCE" in 2 Thessalonians 3:5 is variously translated "the patient waiting for Christ"; "the persistence that Christ manifested"; and "the patience Christ gives us in trials." Perhaps Paul had all three meanings in mind. Certainly Jesus Christ is our great example in patient endurance, not only in the circumstances of His sufferings (Hebrews 12:1–2; Revelation 1:9) but also in His longsuffering with people who were slow to understand His words and trust Him (Luke 9:41). The Thessalonian saints needed steadfastness because they were experiencing severe persecutions and testing (2 Thessalonians 1:4).

When we suffer for the Lord, perseverance depends on patience, and patience and perseverance are products of faith. "Not only so, but we also rejoice in our sufferings, because we know that suffering produces perseverance" (Romans 5:3). "You need to persevere so that when you have done the will of God, you will receive what he has promised" (Hebrews 10:36). God wants us "to imitate those who through faith and patience inherit what has been promised" (Hebrews 6:12). A persevering heart, relying and resting wholly on the Lord, enables us to mature in the Christian life and to draw upon the fullness we have in Christ (James 1:4).

Impatient people usually lack depth, strength, and faith. Faith leads to calmness and quiet waiting; impatience leads to fretting and scheming. Abraham became impatient with God and took Hagar as his wife, and the birth of Ishmael into the household brought a great deal of trouble. Moses became impatient with the people of Israel, called them rebels, and smote the rock instead of speaking to it. He lost the privilege of going into the Promised Land. David became impatient and frightened as Saul pursued him, so he went to the Philistines for protection. He had to lie and pretend to be insane in order to escape.

In times of trial, the Lord can strengthen our hearts if we turn to Him for help, rely on His Word, and wait for His timing (1 Thessalonians 3:13). If we are "firmly established in the truth" (2 Peter 1:12), we will also be firmly established in our hearts and also be able to wait before the Lord with perseverance.

A Hopeful Heart

ONE OF THE GREATEST sources of encouragement in times of temptation and trial is the promise of our Lord's return. "May he strengthen your hearts so that you will be blameless and holy in the presence of our God and Father when our Lord Jesus comes with all his holy ones" (1 Thessalonians 3:13). The blessed hope of Christ's return encourages us to live holy lives so that we will be "unashamed before him at his coming" (1 John 2:28).

Every chapter in 1 Thessalonians ends with a reference to the return of Jesus and the blessings that event will bring. Those who eagerly anticipate Christ's return give evidence that they are truly born again (1 Thessalonians 1:9–10). They also have a strong motivation to serve the Lord and seek to reach others with the gospel (1 Thessalonians 2:19–20). As mentioned before, expecting Jesus to return motivates us to live godly lives (1 Thessalonians 3:13; 5:23–24). It also gives us comfort when our believing loved ones and friends die. We grieve their leaving us, but not as those who have no hope (1 Thessalonians 4:13–18). One day all of us in God's family will be "together with the Lord" and live with the Lord forever. What a blessed hope!

Jesus Christ is "our hope" (1 Timothy 1:1). Those "who have no hope" (1 Thessalonians 4:13) are those who have never received Jesus Christ as their own Lord and Savior, and what a tragic thing it is to live without hope. I have been in the surgical waiting room with unbelieving families when the surgeon has said, "We've done all we can. I'm sorry, there is no hope." That report closed the door to the family's future with that loved one. They had no hope. I have also been with Christian families when they have heard bad news, and even though they were hurting deeply, their response was full of hope. "The best is yet to come! Jesus is coming!" The promise of our Lord's return is not only a happy and holy hope, but it is a healing hope, for the comfort of His coming heals the brokenhearted and assures them that the future is secure. Jesus has gone back to heaven to prepare a place for each of His people, and He will return to take us home.

"Do not let your hearts be troubled" (John 14:1).

CHAPTER 12

THE HOLINESS BENEDICTION

*May God himself, the God of peace, sanctify you through and
through. May your whole spirit, soul and body be kept blameless at the coming of our Lord Jesus Christ. The one who calls
you is faithful and he will do it* (1 Thessalonians 5:23–24).

PAUL WROTE THIS LETTER to young Christian believers and
dared to use the theological word *sanctify*. There are many
Christians today who do not understand the meaning of this
important biblical concept because there is a trend to simplify
Christian vocabulary and turn the Bible into an "easy-reader" book
like those used to teach basic reading skills to children. And yet it is
important for Christians to understand and apply biblical concepts
like *sanctification* so that they can live godly lives.

For example, a missionary told me that in the city where the
Lord has placed him, "the people get saved only from the waist
up." It is necessary that these people read and understand 1 Thessalonians 4:3: "It is God's will that you should be sanctified: that
you should avoid sexual immorality." Clearly the people of this
city need to understand what the inspired word *sanctify* means so
that they can apply the concept and live godly lives.

In some ways, our expectations for young students are high.
Elementary students learn how to use computers and other elec-
tronic devices at school and at home. High school students learn
the vocabulary of chemistry, physics, and other sciences. Even
more important than the vocabularies of science and electronics is
having an understanding of the inspired Christian vocabulary that
tells people how to live godly lives. Understanding and applying

the Christian vocabulary is a key to godly living, so it seems wise for us to learn what these inspired words mean and how we can apply them. This is a reasonable expectation for Christians who desire to live faithfully before God.

To sanctify simply means "to set apart for God's exclusive use." God set apart the tabernacle in the camp of Israel, and the people used it only for those purposes God assigned to it. He sanctified the priests and Levites to perform their ministries. He set apart the seventh day of the week to be used only as He directed. It was to be different from all the other days.

As God's children, we have been set apart as "saints," and we should live like it (2 Thessalonians 2:13–14). Some of the believers in the church of Corinth were not living godly lives, yet Paul addressed them as people "sanctified in Christ Jesus" (1 Corinthians 1:2). Positional sanctification means we are set apart for Jesus Christ, and this never changes; but practical sanctification means that we practice day by day what the Word teaches us, and this can change. Sanctification means glorifying God by living godly lives. Christians are called saints because they have been sanctified, set apart for Jesus. When Jesus returns and we see Him, we will experience perfect sanctification because we shall be like Him (1 John 3:1–3).

It's unfortunate that some people have confused views of the sanctified Christian life.

This benediction presents some blessings of the sanctified life and explains how we may experience them.

An ORDERLY LIFE

I HAVE BEEN in meetings where loud noise and seeming uncontrolled physical activity marked what people considered "sanctified worship." There was no order to the service, and, like the people in the book of Judges, "Every man did what was right in his own eyes" (Judges 17:6; 21:25 NASB). But our God is the God of peace, and while worship can include Spirit-directed enthusiasm, there is no place for confusion or fleshly demonstrations. Paul wrote, "The spirits of prophets are subject to the control of prophets. For God is not a God of disorder but of peace" (1 Corinthians 14:32–33). The word that is translated *disorder* refers to instability and disturbances of various kinds. "For I am afraid that when I come I may not find you as I want you to be . . . I fear there may be quarreling, jealousy, outbursts of anger, factions, slander, gossip, arrogance and disorder" (2 Corinthians 12:20).

It isn't our enthusiastic religious exhibitions in church on Sundays that mark us as God's sanctified people. It's our godly walk and faithful work during the week, letting our light shine in a dark world. It's heeding the apostolic admonition, "Live in peace with each other" (1 Thessalonians 5:13). Read 1 Thessalonians 5:12–22 and you will find a description of the sanctified behavior of God's people as they worship together. Paul explains what it means to be sanctified and to live an orderly life. "For God is not a God of disorder but of peace." Therefore, if our lives are characterized by disorder and confusion, we are not experiencing sanctification.

In the creation narrative, we see the Holy Spirit bringing order out of chaos (Genesis 1), and whenever the Spirit is allowed to work, He will perform that ministry. "For God is not a God of disorder but of peace." Believers who walk in the Spirit will have orderly lives, even though to the unbelieving world their lives may seem inconsistent. Jesus compared the work of the Spirit in the believer to the blowing of the unpredictable wind (John 3:8). The Holy Spirit is infinitely original and doesn't allow consistency to degenerate into dead uniformity. The admonition "Continue to work out your salvation with fear and trembling" (Philippians 2:12) was written to a local congregation, because God desires variety in His church. Unless the Spirit is working in the church, unity soon disappears, and uniformity and legalism will take its place.

An Integrated Life

THE GOD OF PEACE desires not only unity in the church collectively but also wholeness and integrity within each individual believer in the church. Paul called this being sanctified "through and through" and being blameless in our "whole spirit, soul and body." He wants to cooperate with the Holy Spirit in attaining the full limit of our spiritual stature, complete in every part. When Epaphras prayed for the believers in Colosse, he asked that they might "stand firm in all the will of God, mature and fully assured" (Colossians 4:12). The Lord wants us to "become mature, attaining to the whole measure of the fullness of Christ" (Ephesians 4:13). The Spirit-filled life is an integrated life.

A baby whose organs and limbs do not mature harmoniously would end up sadly disabled, unable to enjoy normal activities. The child would survive only with the help of support equipment and constant care. The human body is a masterpiece of design and coordination, but if its many parts get out of balance, the body cannot function properly. To maintain the vital balance of a healthy body, we must avoid danger and defilement, eat properly, practice good hygiene, exercise, and get good rest.

According to Colossians 2:10, "in Him you have been made complete" (NASB), which the *Living Bible* paraphrases, "So you have everything when you have Christ." When we were born again through faith in Christ, we were "born complete in Him," with "everything we need for life and godliness" (2 Peter 1:3). It would be strange if the parents of a newborn baby had to return to the hospital week after week to get new "parts" for their child. Praise God when children are born complete and have the God-given capacity for balanced development! So God desires that His children be "mature and complete, not lacking anything" (James 1:4). Paul admonished Timothy, "Train yourself to be godly," and the word that is translated *train* gives us our English word *gymnasium*. It's interesting to see how many athletic terms Paul used in his letters, for both the Greeks and the Romans (like people today) were passionately caught up in athletics.

God wants us to be sanctified "through and through," and not just in one area of the Christian life. Our times alone with the Lord in prayer and worship need to be balanced with times when we fellowship with God's people and seek to serve them for the Lord. But we need to be with unconverted people also and seek to influence them for the Lord. Dr. Harry Ironside used to summarize the book of Hebrews with two balanced phrases: "within the veil" (Hebrews 6:19 KJV) and "without the camp" (Hebrews 13:13 KJV). "Within the veil" describes our private fellowship with the Lord, and it alludes to the high priest entering the Holy of Holies in the tabernacle; and "without the camp" describes our ministry to a lost world, just as Jesus suffered on the cross outside Jerusalem. We need to balance rejoicing in the Lord and being rejected by the world. Both are part of the normal Christian life and help us to grow toward maturity in Jesus.

The phrase "spirit, soul and body" reminds us that both the outer and the inner person must be given to the Lord to experience His sanctifying power. In Romans 8:10, Paul speaks of "body and spirit" (see also 1 Corinthians 5:5; 7:34; and 2 Corinthians 7:1), and sometimes Paul speaks only of the heart (1 Thessalonians 3:13; 2 Thessalonians 2:16–17 and 3:5). Moses in Deuteronomy 6:5 commands us to love the Lord with all of our heart, soul, and strength. When Jesus quoted this verse, He said heart, soul, mind and strength (Mark 12:30; Luke 10:27). According to Hebrews 4:12, there is a difference between the soul and the spirit, and it's only through the Word that we can distinguish between a "soulish" life and a spiritual life.

Apparently Paul was not arguing for any particular view of human personality. The Bible challenges God's children to give their all to the Lord—body, mind, heart, will, soul, spirit, and strength—and allow the Spirit of God to set apart the total person for His service and to His glory. There are sins of the flesh and of the spirit (2 Corinthians 7:1). The prodigal son was guilty of the first and his elder brother of the second, and both grieved their father. When we ask the Spirit to fill us (control us), He works in and through every facet of our personality to integrate each part with the total person so that we have wholeness.

An Exemplary Life

IN THIS LIFE, nobody can be sinless, but we can be blameless—that is, free from accusation.

The Greek scholar Richard Trench defined being blameless as "the absence of blemish and of blame" (*Synonyms of the New Testament*, 354). When a child draws a picture, it isn't perfect, but if it's the best he or she can do, then the picture is blameless. The test of our lives isn't what we think about ourselves or what other people think of us, but what God will say when we stand before Him. The Lord wants us to be blameless when we see Jesus (1 Corinthians 1:8; Colossians 1:22), which means that right now our lives must be "holy, righteous and blameless" (1 Thessalonians 2:10). It means exercising spiritual discernment (Philippians 1:10) and separating ourselves from the defilement of this world (Philippians 2:15).

"For we will all stand before God's judgment seat" (Romans 14:10). "For we must all appear before the judgment seat of Christ, that each one may receive what is due him for the things done while in the body, whether good or bad" (2 Corinthians 5:10). This is not the judgment described in Revelation 20:13–15, which is reserved for lost sinners to determine their degree of punishment. It is a judgment of believers to determine the rewards they will receive on the basis of the lives they have led and the works they have done. God doesn't hold our sins against us (Hebrews 10:17–18; Romans 8:1), but our disobedience affects our character and our works. We don't want to be like Lot and see everything we have lived for burn up (1 Corinthians 3:12–15).

The promised return of Christ should motivate us to live blamelessly in this present evil age. "I am coming soon. Hold on to what you have, so that no one will take your crown" (Revelation 3:11). How easy it is for us to be deceived and think that we (and others) are ready to meet the Lord and have our works judged. "Therefore judge nothing before the appointed time; wait till the Lord comes. He will bring to light what is hidden in darkness and will expose the motives of men's hearts. At that time each will receive his praise from God" (1 Corinthians 4:5). "And now, dear children, continue in him, so that when he appears we may be confident and unashamed before him at his coming" (1 John 2:28).

Living an exemplary life today not only prepares us for the judgment seat of Christ, but it also enables us to witness to the lost and prepare them for the future. "You are the light of the world," said Jesus. "Let your light shine before men, that they may see your good deeds and praise your Father in heaven" (Matthew 5:14, 16). Paul and his helpers had lived blamelessly before the Thessalonian believers (1 Thessalonians 2:10–12); therefore, he looked forward to seeing them in heaven one day where he would give glory to the Lord because of them (1 Thessalonians 2:19–20). No matter how much discouragement and difficulty may come our way as we serve the Lord, if we are faithful the future will bring its rewards and glorify the Lord.

An Empowered Life

"The one who calls you is faithful and he will do it." What an encouragement!

By God's power we can "live lives worthy of God, who calls you into his kingdom and glory" (1 Thessalonians 2:12). You can be "confident of this, that he who began a good work in you will carry it on to completion until the day of Christ Jesus" (Philippians 1:6). Jesus is the "author and perfecter of our faith" (Hebrews 12:2), and He will never forsake us (Hebrews 13:5). Not only does the Father

Himself sanctify us, but so do the Son (Ephesians 5:25–27) and the Holy Spirit (2 Thessalonians 2:13; Romans 15:16). They use the Word of God to transform our lives and make us more like Jesus Christ (John 17:17; 2 Corinthians 3:18; 2 Thessalonians 2:13).

Just as Paul prayed for the sanctification of the new believers in Thessalonica, we can pray for others—and for ourselves—that the image of Christ might more and more be revealed in our lives. Whether the burden is for careless church members, wayward family members, or believers going through great trials, we have the privilege and obligation to pray that God would change their lives. When we're going through trials, the important thing isn't *that* we get out of them but *what* we get out of them. What a tragedy it is to waste our suffering and not benefit from our pain.

We can have confidence that God will work on our behalf because His relationship to us is wholly of grace. It's part of His calling. "For God did not call us to be impure, but to live a holy life" (1 Thessalonians 4:7). "He called you to this through our gospel, that you might share in the glory of our Lord Jesus Christ" (2 Thessalonians 2:14). God did not call us because of our godly character or good works, because we were sinners, deserving of judgment. He called us because of His love and grace. God's calling always includes God's enabling, and we can trust Him to empower us to do His will and fulfill His purposes as we yield to Him (Philippians 2:12–13).

Note that the verb in 1 Thessalonians 5:24 is present tense—actually, a present participle, which implies continuing action: "the one who *calls* you." God in His grace called us to salvation, and now He continues to call us to experience a godly life. Whenever we read the Word and pray, whenever we worship and fellowship with godly people, whenever we receive some special blessing, it is God calling us again to a life of holiness and obedience. *And God is faithful to do what He has commanded.* "He will keep you strong to the end, so that you will be blameless on the day of our Lord

Jesus Christ. God, who has called you into fellowship with his Son Jesus Christ our Lord, is faithful" (1 Corinthians 1:8–9). "But the Lord is faithful, and he will strengthen and protect you from the evil one" (2 Thessalonians 3:3). Jesus is a "merciful and faithful high priest" (Hebrews 2:17), and, "He who promised is faithful" (Hebrews 10:23).

God does not work in spite of us or instead of us; He works in us and through us. We "reign in life through the one man, Jesus Christ" (Romans 5:17). This means that we sit on the throne together (Ephesians 2:6), and we share His power and authority as we submit to His will. Knowing that He is faithful and able to do all that must be done, we have quiet confidence that there is nothing to worry about. Like the three friends of Daniel, we can boldly say, "The God we serve is able" (Daniel 3:17). As Paul wrote, "The one who calls you is faithful and he will do it"(1 Thessalonians 5:24). He has the power to keep us going and to see us through.

The motive that compels us to obey God and live holy lives is not fear of judgment or the terror of law. It is His grace, revealed in Jesus Christ and displayed on the cross. Charles Haddon Spurgeon said, "The law which you think would drive men to holiness has never done it, while the grace which you imagine would lead us to licentiousness binds us with solemn bands of consecration to serve our God ten times more than before" (*The Metropolitan Tabernacle Pulpit*, vol. 19, 93).

> O to grace how great a debtor
> Daily I'm constrained to be!
> Let thy goodness, like a fetter,
> Bind my wandering heart to Thee.
> Prone to wander, Lord, I feel it,
> Prone to leave the God I love;
> Here's my heart, O take and seal it,
> Seal it for Thy courts above.
>
> —Robert Robbins

CHAPTER 13

THE ENCOURAGEMENT
BENEDICTION

*May our Lord Jesus Christ himself and God our Father, who
loved us and by his grace gave us eternal encouragement and
good hope, encourage your hearts and strengthen you in every
good deed and word* (2 Thessalonians 2:16–17).

THE FIRST EXPERIENCES of Paul's Christian life were anything
but encouraging (Acts 9:1–31). His enemies in Damascus
threatened to kill him, so he had to be smuggled out of the city
in a basket lowered over the wall. When Paul arrived in Jerusalem,
the apostles weren't sure he was a believer, let alone an apostle, and
Barnabas ("the Son of Encouragement"—Acts 4:36) had to open
the doors for him. With a friend like Barnabas, Paul learned to be
an encourager early in his ministry, and he kept it up to the end.
In fact, all of us should be encouragers. As the British preacher
John Watson said, "Be kind, for everyone you meet is fighting a
battle."

Discouragement has probably weakened and destroyed more
ministries than any other enemy of the faith. "A cheerful heart is
good medicine, but a crushed spirit dries up the bones" (Proverbs
17:22). Many believers don't see discouragement as a sin to be immediately confessed to the Lord, so they hang on to it too long and
it grows worse. When we're discouraged, it usually means we're
walking by sight and not by faith. "In this world you will have
trouble," Jesus told His disciples. "But take heart! I have overcome
the world" (John 16:33).

Our English word *courage* comes from the Latin *cor* through the French *coer*, both of which mean "heart." To be discouraged means "to lose heart"; to be encouraged means "to strengthen the heart." The Greek word *paraklesis* is translated comfort, consolation, or encouragement, and it gives us one of the names of the Holy Spirit, *parakletos* (or Paraclete), which is translated "helper," "comforter," "counselor," and "encourager." The Holy Spirit is to believers today what Jesus was to His disciples when He was with them on earth—teacher, encourager, helper. "You, dear children, are from God and have overcome them, because the one who is in you is greater than the one who is in the world" (1 John 4:4). Believers carry within themselves a power greater than anything the world can produce. What an encouragement!

As you read your Bible, please note that even some of the great saints of the past had their dark hours of discouragement. Consider Moses (Numbers 11:1–15), Joshua (Joshua 7), David (1 Samuel 27), Elijah (1 Kings 19), the prophet Jeremiah (Jeremiah 15:10; 20:1ff), and even some of the early believers who had known Jesus in the flesh (Luke 24:13–35). When I was a young believer and attended conferences, I was sure the speakers I heard lived constantly on the mountain peaks of faith and never saw any clouds. Then the Lord called me into conference ministry, and I was privileged to minister with some of these "giants" and get to know them better, and that's when I discovered the truth. They had battles and burdens just like the rest of us, and sometimes they were under the dark clouds of discouragement and praying for the Lord to show His face. As I read biographies and autobiographies, I learned that the giants of church history were men and women of clay like the rest of us.

When we find ourselves suddenly or gradually moving under a cloud of discouragement, we need to remember three privileges we have in the Lord, give thanks for them, meditate on them, and let God minister to us so we can minister to others.

THE RELATIONSHIPS WE ENJOY

THE LITTLE WORD *our* reminds us that we have a Father and a
Savior in heaven who love us—*and they are ours!* "*Our* Lord Jesus
Christ . . . *our* Father." We can say with the Shulamite maiden,
"My beloved is mine, and I am his" (Song of Songs 2:16 NKJV),
and we can pray from our hearts, "Our Father in heaven" (Mat-
thew 6:9). No matter how uncomfortable or threatening the cir-
cumstances around us or the distress within us, our Father is still
in control, and our Savior will never forsake us (Hebrews 13:5).
Discouragement often puts us in front of the mirror, and we spend
so much time looking at ourselves that we forget to look to the
Lord. We feel sorry for ourselves and forget to give thanks to the
Father and the Son for their manifold mercies.

It's worth noting that 1 Thessalonians 2:16 has a plural subject
("our Lord Jesus Christ himself and God our Father"), but the verbs
in verses 16–17 are all singular in the original text. This means that
Paul fully accepted the deity of Jesus Christ and put Him on an
equal status with the Father. We must never think that the Son loves
us more than the Father does, because they are one in their love,
their plans, and their work (John 10:30; 14:9–10; 17:23, 26).

When people are sick, they don't want to read a medical book;
they want to see a physician. When there are legal problems, they
want to consult a lawyer. If an appliance is broken, they search the
yellow pages for a specialist who makes house calls. So with the
burdens of life: we want a Father and a Savior to help us accept the
situation, understand it better, and know what to do about it. Instead of looking back with regret, or looking within and conduct-
ing a painful autopsy, we ought to look up by faith to the Father
and the Son *who are ours.*

In times of despair we often feel guilty and question whether
God still loves us, but God's love is there just the same. Sometimes we try to negotiate with the Lord and bargain with Him to
"make everything right," but that means moving out of grace into

law—and it doesn't work. That approach only increases guilt and makes things worse. Jesus loved the family in Bethany, but Lazarus still got sick and died, and Jesus delayed coming to see Mary and Martha. God the Father loves His Son, but He still willed that Jesus suffer and die on a cross.

We don't measure God's love by the way we feel or by the directions that circumstances take. We measure the love of the Father and the Son by what they say in the Word and what they did at Calvary. "But God demonstrates his own love for us in this: While we were still sinners, Christ died for us" (Romans 5:8). This love isn't just a doctrinal fact written in the Bible; it's a personal experience. "And hope does not disappoint us, because God has poured out his love into our hearts by the Holy Spirit, whom he has given us" (Romans 5:5). "If anyone loves me, he will obey my teaching. My Father will love him, and we will come to him and make our home with him" (John 14:23).

Some may ask, "Why doesn't Paul include the Holy Spirit— the Encourager—along with the Father and the Son?" Let Charles Spurgeon answer the question: "The Holy Spirit is the Comforter, but *Christ is the comfort*" (*The Metropolitan Tabernacle Pulpit*, vol. 40, 257). The Spirit doesn't reveal Himself; He reveals Jesus Christ and glorifies Him. And the better we know the Son, the better we know the Father. (See John 14:9; 16:14.) If we are truly filled with the Spirit and walking in the Spirit, Jesus will become more and more real to us and give us the encouragement that we need. When we magnify the Holy Spirit and ignore Jesus, the Spirit may be grieved; but when we glorify Jesus Christ, the Spirit is pleased.

We are encouraged not only by our relationship with the Father and Son in heaven but also by our relationships with the people of God here on earth. Paul wrote to his Thessalonian friends and prayed for them, and this made a difference in their lives. God often ministers His love and care to us by the Holy Spirit working in and through the people around us. In one of his darkest hours, when he was almost ready to give up, Paul found encouragement in the arrival of Titus and the good news he brought from the believers at Corinth (2 Corinthians 1:8–10; 7:5–7). After enduring two weeks in a storm that ended in shipwreck and then three months on Malta, Paul finally arrived at Rome, where a group of the believers met him. "At the sight of these men Paul thanked God and was encouraged" (Acts 28:15). Imagine encouraging a miracle-working apostle!

Difficulties can lead to discouragement, and discouragement can result in despair, but the presence of God's people, along with their words and prayers, can make a great difference. "The one thing we remember most about our former pastor and his wife," a church officer said to me, "was that they were always there. No matter what time, day or night, they were right there with us, praying for us and sharing the Word of God." We don't have to make speeches or attempt to explain the situation. Just "being there" is an encouragement to others, and the Spirit can work through us to bring peace and confidence to their hearts.

In the paragraph preceding his benediction, Paul reminded his readers of what the Lord had done for them (2 Thessalonians 2:13–15). The Lord loved them and chose them, and the Spirit set them apart to receive salvation. God sent Paul to call them through his preaching of the gospel, and they believed and were saved. No matter what they had to endure as believers, one day they would share the glory of Jesus Christ. In the light of these marvelous blessings, they had every reason to "stand firm and hold to the teachings" Paul had given to them. Then Paul prayed for them, that God's encouragement would fill their hearts. "The preacher's work is only half done when he has exhorted his hearers to stand fast; he must then fall upon his knees and pray for them," said Charles Spurgeon (*Metropolitan Tabernacle Pulpit*, vol. 52, 278). That's a good example for us to follow.

THE RICHES WE POSSESS

THE FATHER HAS GIVEN to us in Jesus Christ all that we need for Christian life and service (2 Peter 1:3), and Paul named five of these blessings: love, grace, eternal encouragement, good hope, and spiritual strength. How rich we are! Why should we be discouraged?

Love. In 1 Thessalonians 1:4 and 2 Thessalonians 2:13, Paul addressed the believers as people "loved by the Lord." From our point of view, God's love was the starting point of our salvation experience. "We love because he first loved us" (1 John 4:19). To quote Spurgeon again: "To hear of the love of God is sweet—to believe it most precious—but to enjoy it is Paradise below" (*The Metropolitan Tabernacle Pulpit,* vol. 19, 86). Too many Christians talk and sing about the love of God, but they don't really experience it in their own hearts. We hear 1 Corinthians 13 solemnly read at weddings and funerals and forget that the chapter was written for us to enjoy and experience every day of the year. Every Christian grace we need is a by-product of God's love. No matter what we experience in life, pleasant or painful, we can be sure it comes from the loving heart of our heavenly Father.

Grace. Mercy means we don't receive from God what we do deserve, and grace means we do receive from Him what we don't deserve. Paul opened his letter with *grace* and closed it with *grace,* a reminder to his readers and to us that the Christian life is *grace* from the beginning to end. The "riches of his grace" will never be depleted or devalued (Ephesians 2:7), and "the God of all grace" (1 Peter 5:10) is ready to provide what we need.

Eternal encouragement. Another translation is "eternal comfort," but don't limit this blessing to our life in heaven. It's not likely that we will need comfort in heaven since we will have glorified bodies in the heavenly city. "Unfailing consolation" is a good translation. In other words, we can experience the comforts of heaven today. It has well been said, "Little faith will take your soul to heaven, but great faith will bring heaven to your soul." Our citizenship is in heaven (Philippians 3:20–21), our Father is in heaven (Matthew 6:9), our High Priest is in heaven (Hebrews 8:1), and our home is in heaven (John 14:1–6), and we can enjoy some of heaven's blessings today because we are seated with Christ in the heavenlies (Ephesians 2:6–7). We have the comforts of heaven to enable us as we face the conflicts on earth.

Good hope. At the time Paul wrote his two letters to the believers in Thessalonica, the church was upset about their future and the future of those believers who had already died (2 Thessalonians 2:1ff). The hope of the return of Christ had inspired their endurance in persecution (1 Thessalonians 1:3), but now that endurance was being threatened. God's people may disagree over the details of future events, but they solidly agree that when Jesus said, "I will come back" (John 14:3), He really meant it. Not only is it a good hope, but it is also a joyful hope (Romans 12:12), a blessed hope (Titus 2:13) and a living hope (1 Peter 1:3). The world gives birth to hopes that live for a short time and then die, but our hope of seeing Jesus is alive and gets greater every day. Alas, most of all the people in this world are "without hope" (Ephesians 2:12; 1 Thessalonians 4:13) because they have never heard the gospel and trusted Jesus Christ, or they have heard the salvation message and refused to believe.

Strength. The circumstances may not change, but God can still give us the strength within to confront them and keep on going. "O, do not pray for easy lives," said Phillips Brooks. "Pray to be stronger men! Do not pray for tasks equal to your powers. Pray for powers equal to your tasks" (William Scarlett, ed., *Selected Sermons of Phillips Brooks,* p. 344). Gideon said he couldn't lead an army, but God said He would help him, and with only three hundred men, Gideon defeated the enemy. Just about the time our strength is at its lowest, the Lord moves in with His divine power and the job gets done. "God chose the weak things of the world to shame the strong" (1 Corinthians 1:27). By faith, yield to the Lord and ask for His power, and if your desire is to glorify Him, He will meet the need.

These are but a few of the riches we possess in Christ, riches that are available to us no matter what the test. Every challenge we face is an opportunity for us to discover the wealth of God's grace and the blessing of glorifying Him in our weakness. We learn what Paul meant when he wrote, "For when I am weak, then I am strong" (2 Corinthians 12:10). So when discouragement begins to infect your spiritual life, pause and take inventory of the wealth God has already given to you and the wealth that still remains for you to share. Forget about what you don't have and give thanks for what you do have, trusting God to supply your every need. Read your Bible and discover the riches you have in Christ Jesus and how the Spirit of God can impart them to you. The Spirit is the Encourager, and He will never fail you if you trust Him.

THE RESPONSiBiLiTiES WE ACCEPT

WHY SHOULD GOD encourage us and strengthen our hearts? So that we may be comfortable and happy? No, He does it so that we may be able to serve others by what we do and what we say, our works and our words. The British Anglican pastor and poet John Keble (1792–1866) wrote to a troubled friend, "When you find yourself overpowered as it were by melancholy, the best way is to go out and do something kind to somebody or other" (*Letters of Spiritual Counsel*, R. F. Wilson, ed., 6). When we think only of ourselves, we become like reservoirs cluttered with sludge and garbage, but when we think of others and serve them, we become like pure flowing rivers of living water (John 7:37–38).

Paul begins with our deeds because our words mean nothing if our lives don't glorify the Lord. Christians are to be recognized by their godly lives, not just by their religious words. Paul admonishes us "that those who have trusted in God . . . be careful to devote themselves to doing what is good" (Titus 3:8). We have been "created in Christ Jesus to do good works, which God prepared in advance for us to do" (Ephesians 2:10). Our good works are like shining lights that point people to God (Matthew 5:14–16).

But good works are not simply church work, because serving Christians find many opportunities to glorify God by helping others, especially those outside the church. It's to the praise of the Lord that concerned Christians contributed to achievements in prison reform, the care of orphans, child labor reform, the abolition of slavery, and the promotion of education. In every community there are people and organizations outside the church that need the help of devoted believers from inside the church, starting with those in our own neighborhood. Unemployed young people can serve God in their summer vacation months by helping the elderly, the handicapped, unsupervised children, and even the city park district. There is always a task to fulfill for those who want to let their lights shine.

Busy people are usually happy people; the idle think too much about themselves and wait for others to serve them. Why do we promote service overseas and ignore service at home? Both are important, and the work at home is great preparation for service elsewhere. I have been privileged to serve on several mission boards, and I would not recommend a candidate who had done nothing to serve others here at home. Dr. Oswald J. Smith used to say, "The light that shines the farthest will shine the brightest at home." He was right.

Once our works are pleasing to the Lord, we have earned the right to share our words and tell others about Christ. *Never underestimate the power of words spoken from a heart of love, backed by a life of service.* The ability to use words is one of God's special gifts to us, and it must not be neglected or abused. Never underestimate the power of words. American writer and author Norman Cousins observed that for every word in Adolph Hitler's book, *Mein Kampf,* 125 people died in World War II.

The book of Proverbs emphasizes the awesome power of words wisely chosen and lovingly spoken. Wise and just words are compared to gold and silver (10:20; 25:11–12). What we say either enriches people or cheapens them. Right words are like refreshing streams to the thirsty (10:11; 13:14; 18:4) and nourishing food to the hungry (15:4; 16:24). A sharp tongue can cut and hurt, but wise words are like medicine that brings healing (Proverbs 12:14, 18; 13:2). Where there is war, a loving tongue can help to bring peace (15:1, 18), and where there is sin, a loving rebuke can help to save a straying soul (10:17; 25:12; 28:23). An encouraging word can help the burdened (12:25; 15:23; 16:24). Most of all, a loving witness backed by a godly life can lead sinners to trust Jesus Christ (14:25; 24:11–12; see Acts 1:8). "The tongue has the power of life and death" (Proverbs 18:21), and it is up to us to use speech to impart life and love.

Before I leave this theme, let me remind you that written words can in some ways be more effective than spoken words. For one thing, they are permanent and can be read over and over. A greeting card and a brief note sent to the elderly or the shut-in can bring that ray of light so badly needed. How I thank God for believers who use e-mail to send a word of encouragement to missionaries and friends in difficult places! God has given us marvelous tools for communicating love and truth rapidly and economically, so let's use them for His glory.

Behind a smiling face is often a broken heart. Let's listen carefully, use discernment, and speak words that will sustain the weary (Isaiah 50:4–5). It's one of the greatest ministries we can have.

CHAPTER 14

THE PEACE BENEDICTION

Now may the Lord of peace himself give you peace at all times and in every way. The Lord be with all of you (2 Thessalonians 3:16).

THE SCOTTISH PREACHER George Morrison defined peace as "the possession of adequate resources." If there's enough money in the checking account, you don't fret when the mail carrier delivers bills. If the cupboard and refrigerator are stocked, you don't worry about unexpected guests arriving. If the children are getting good grades in school, you feel confident about financial aid and scholarships. But these earthly resources are nothing when compared with the spiritual resources we have in Jesus Christ, and it's the spiritual that really counts. God is more than adequate and able to handle any challenges that come our way, and that assurance is the source of our peace.

However, many people in this world are experiencing a false peace that has lulled them into a dangerous sleep. "While people are saying, 'Peace and safety,' destruction will come on them suddenly, as labor pains on a pregnant woman, and they will not escape" (1 Thessalonians 5:3). Jesus said, "Peace I leave with you; my peace I give you. I do not give to you as the world gives. Do not let your hearts be troubled and do not be afraid" (John 14:27). The peace the world offers is a temporary distraction, not a permanent possession. It's usually based on deception, not reality, and never really solves the problems in the heart. Until we are right with God and have His peace within, we can never be right with ourselves, our circumstances, or with other people. Before we can enjoy "the peace of God" (Philippians 4:7), we must have "peace with God" through faith in Jesus Christ (Romans 5:10).

Our benediction reveals some important facts about the "Lord of all peace" and the peace that He gives His children.

ONLY FROM THE LORD

THE WORLD OFFERS medications and treatments for those who are troubled, and while we can buy a temporary fix for anxiety, we can't buy peace. And yet peace is what we desperately need, for without peace, we are vulnerable in this warring world. Just as health demands a proper balance in the mind and body, so the Christian's inner person must have the "balance" that comes from possessing the peace of God. Normal spiritual growth is difficult if not impossible when we lack this peace. Furthermore, how can we be witnesses in a nervous and frightened world if our own lives are anxious and upset? To be impulsive or stubborn is to imitate "the horse or the mule" (Psalm 32:9) and to lose the peace of God.

God's peace is not the absence of conflict but the satisfying presence of the Lord in the midst of our battles. We usually ask God to change our difficult circumstances, but our Father wants to use those circumstances to make us more like Jesus Christ; "Conformed to the likeness of his Son" is what Paul called it (Romans 8:29). *That's why Paul could boldly say that "in all things God works for the good of those who love him"* (Romans 8:28). In order to accomplish God's will, Jesus had to suffer and die, and if we want to become like Jesus, we must have our share of pain and challenges. But the Lord doesn't share His peace with us the way a physician gives us a pill or a shot of medicine in the arm. "You will keep in perfect peace him whose mind is steadfast, because he trusts in you" (Isaiah 26:3). That means faith fixed on the Lord. You find a similar formula in Philippians 4:6–9: a heart devoted to prayer and gratitude and a mind devoted to the right kind of thinking. When the heart and mind are saturated with the Word and focused on

Jesus Christ, then the Spirit helps us obey the Lord's command, "Do not let your hearts be troubled" (John 14:1, 27). The heart of the worry problem is the problem of the heart, and only God's peace can change the heart.

When some people find themselves disturbed and afraid, they might swallow a pill or turn on the TV set and get distracted. Or they might phone a friend and talk about their worries. But when the medication wears off, the television program is over, and the telephone conversation ends, the anxiety is still in their heart, and their circumstances haven't improved. Peace that comes from temporary distraction only makes the problems worse. God's children can have a permanent peace within if they keep their eyes on the Lord, pray, and fill their hearts and minds with His promises.

"The Lord of peace" is also called "the God of peace" (Romans 15:33; 16:20; 2 Corinthians 13:11; Philippians 4:9; and 1 Thessalonians 5:23). Note that the entire Godhead is identified with peace: the Father (1 Thessalonians 5:23; Philippians 4:7, 9); the Son (Isaiah 9:6–7; John 14:27; 16:33; 20:19, 21, 26; Ephesians 2:14) and the Holy Spirit (Galatians 5:22).

ONLY AS A GIFT

"Now MAY THE Lord of peace himself give you peace." The believers in Thessalonica desperately needed the peace of God. They were experiencing persecution for their faith. They had been deceived by a false prophecy (2 Thessalonians 2:1–4), and because of that prophecy, some of the people in the church had quit their jobs and were idly waiting for Jesus to return. They were living off the labors of others and creating problems. It was a difficult time for the church, and only the Lord could help them change.

God's peace, of course, is a Person—the Lord Jesus Christ. "For he himself is our peace," wrote Paul (Ephesians 2:14), and the prophet Micah wrote, "And he will be their peace" (5:5). When Jesus was born at Bethlehem, the angels announced, "Glory to

God in the highest, and on earth peace to men on whom his favor rests" (Luke 2:14). But as Jesus approached the cross, He said, "Do you think I came to bring peace on earth? No, I tell you, but division" (Luke 12:51). When we trust the Savior, we have peace in heaven, and we experience peace on earth. But this is peace in the midst of conflict, for the lost world hates Jesus and those who follow Him (John 7:7; 15:18–25; 17:14).

To receive God's peace is to welcome God's Son to the throne of our lives (Romans 5:17), for He is the peace that we need. His first words to His disciples after His resurrection were, "Peace be with you" (John 20:19, 21). Jesus Christ is all that we need, for in Him is everything required for a godly life and ministry. He is our wisdom and power, our righteousness, holiness, and redemption (1 Corinthians 1:24, 30–31). If you had to provide a gift that everybody in the world needed, what would it be? The answer is the gift that the Father gave—Jesus Christ, His Son (John 3:16). We don't deserve this gift; we can't earn it or purchase it. It comes only through the grace of God.

"Ask and it will be given to you" (Luke 11:9).

At All Times and in All Circumstances

"I BELIEVE IT IS peace for our time," said British Prime Minister Neville Chamberlain on September 30, 1938, having just returned from Germany where he signed a pact with Adolph Hitler. But Chamberlain's faith proved to be fantasy, for Hitler proceeded to break his promises, continue his conquests, and eventually bring the world into war. The peace that Jesus gives us is not for one time or for our time only but for all time and in all circumstances. The phrase can be translated "in all turnings of events." People who base their peace on circumstances quickly find that their peace doesn't last. Circumstances change, people's smiles turn to frowns, the clouds hide the sun, and all our best efforts seem to fail. The American poet Henry Wadsworth Longfellow wrote, "Into each life some rain must fall," and sometimes that rain ushers in a long and difficult storm.

As I read the Bible, I find great encouragement in seeing how the Lord helps His people in the varied situations of life. Moses had peace in his heart when Israel stood at the Red Sea, not knowing how to escape the Egyptian army. When his own people challenged his leadership and defied him, Moses kept calm and trusted God to vindicate Him, as He did. The Lord led David "beside quiet waters" (Psalm 23:2) when he was moving from place to place, and Saul wanted to kill him. Daniel's three friends were at peace when they refused to bow to the idol but faced being burned in the furnace. Whenever I read Acts 25–28, I admire the poise of the apostle Paul as he faced angry mobs, boldly witnessed to powerful rulers, and even went through a terrible storm that wrecked the ship. When the passengers and sailors despaired of life, Paul calmly told them what Jesus had done for him; and because of Paul, the Lord spared all the people on the ship.

We're prone to say, "Lord, this is only a minor matter, so I can take care of it." But those "minor matters" have a way of becoming gigantic problems, and then we wish we had turned to the Lord sooner. When we finally turn to Him, He is always there and well able to handle the circumstances. Whether like Joseph we're sitting in jail, like David facing a giant, or like Peter walking on the water in a storm, the Lord says to us, "Take courage! It is I! Don't be afraid" (Matthew 14:27). The Lord of peace gives us peace no matter what the circumstances might be.

FOR ALL OF GOD'S PEOPLE

THERE IS A BRAND of theology that suggests that God's best blessings are reserved only for the "super saints" whom He has chosen and not for the rest of us, but this theology is wrong. If Jesus is our Lord and Savior, then everything He is and everything He promises belong to all of us, and by faith we can draw upon His fullness. Yes,

God does call some people to special ministries, but we must never think that we are second-class citizens in the kingdom because we are "ordinary people" doing "ordinary work." Most of God's work today is being transacted by faithful people whose names will never be in the headlines, people the leaders depend on to get the work done.

Take time to read 1 Thessalonians 5:1–22; 2 Thessalonians 2:1–4; and 3:6–15 and you will understand better why Paul put such an emphasis on peace. With persecution from the outside and confusion on the inside, the young believers in Thessalonica were experiencing conflict and division. Some of them weren't showing proper respect for their spiritual leaders. Others had foolishly believed a counterfeit "message from the Lord," saying that they were already living in the "day of the Lord" and that the coming of Christ was near, and, as mentioned, some believers had actually stopped working and were doing nothing but waiting for the Lord. Admonitions like "encourage the timid" and "help the weak" (1 Thessalonians 5:14) suggest that some believers weren't maturing in the Lord or boldly stepping out by faith to confront the demands of life. They had to be pampered and sheltered and were a burden to the church.

Talk about a troubled church family! But the peace of God was available to all of them if they would only abandon their false views of life and reach out by faith to the God of peace.

WE CAN SHARE WITH OTHERS

THE BALANCED CHRISTIAN life involves both giving and receiving. God gives that we might receive, and we receive so that we might be able to give. "What do you have that you did not receive?" asked Paul (1 Corinthians 4:7), and John the Baptist said, "A person can receive only what is given from heaven" (John 3:27 TNIV). Whether we believe and obey them, the words of Jesus still stand: "It is more blessed to give than to receive" (Acts 20:35).

When we give to others with the right spirit, we are actually giving to the Lord, and He will see to it that we receive the dividends marked out for us (Matthew 25:34–40). One thing is for sure: nobody can out-give God.

In this world there are too many troublemakers and not enough peacemakers, but we who belong to Jesus must be peacemakers because we are the children of God. "Blessed are the peacemakers, for they will be called sons of God" (Matthew 5:9). The spiritual armor we wear includes the shoes of peace (Ephesians 6:15), which means that we are soldiers who wage peace instead of waging war. Like the armies of Israel when they entered Canaan, we wage war against evil only that we might bring peace to the land; and we battle using the spiritual weapons God has provided (2 Corinthians 10:1–6). During many years of ministry, I have met men and women whose presence brought peace and whose words made that peace even more evident. "There is deceit in the hearts of those who plot evil, but joy for those who promote peace" (Proverbs 12:20). However, we must never compromise the truth and promote "peace at any price," for the true peace is based on righteousness. "But the wisdom that comes from heaven is first of all pure; then peace-loving" (James 3:17–18).

Dedicated Christians should share God's peace, whether entering or leaving a place (Matthew 10:11–13; Luke 10:5–7), and we should send God's faithful servants away with "the blessing of peace" (Acts 15:33). "Send [Timothy] on his way in peace," Paul commanded the saints in Corinth (1 Corinthians 16:11), and "Go in peace" were familiar words in Jewish life (1 Samuel 1:17; 1 Samuel 20:42; Mark 5:34; Luke 7:50). Of course, the mere words "Go in peace" must never be substitutes for the practical help that people need (James 2:14–17). Hospitality to the peace of God is a valid test of whether people will receive the Word and us, and we can sense in our hearts when people don't want the things of Jesus.

In 1969, the Beatles recorded a song entitled "Give Peace a Chance," with this refrain: "All we are saying is give peace a chance." Politically, peace is indeed a chancy thing, but spiritually, peace is a sure thing if the Prince of Peace reigns in our hearts. In today's world, it's either "Go to pieces" or "Go in peace," and God's people can help to make the difference. The prayer attributed to St. Francis of Assisi begins with, "Lord, make me an instrument of Your peace," and that's a great prayer for us daily.

CHAPTER 15

THE SHEPHERD BENEDICTION

May the God of peace, who through the blood of the eternal covenant brought back from the dead our Lord Jesus, that great Shepherd of the sheep, equip you with everything good for doing his will, and may he work in us what is pleasing to him, through Jesus Christ, to whom be glory for ever and ever. Amen (Hebrews 13:20–21).

EVER SINCE THE CONFERENCE recorded in Acts 15, people have been trying to "Judaize" the church and mix the law of Moses with the grace of Jesus Christ. These men in the early church wanted the churches to require Gentile believers to keep the Mosaic law and the Jewish traditions. In Acts 21, we learn that from their viewpoint, believing Gentiles had to become Jews before they could become Christians. Paul answered them powerfully in his epistle to the Galatians, and the author of the epistle to the Hebrews explained further the believer's freedom from the bondage of the Mosaic ceremonial law. The church does not *have* a priesthood; the church *is* a priesthood. Our High Priest is serving in the heavenly sanctuary, and we bring "spiritual sacrifices" to the Lord (Hebrews 8:1–2; 13:15–16; 1 Peter 2:5).

In our day, people want to impose complicated calendars and ceremonies on the simplicity of the Christian faith. The eminent Bible teacher Dr. Donald Grey Barnhouse used to say, "The Book of Hebrews was written to the Hebrews to tell them to quit being Hebrews." Of course, the writer wasn't telling Christian Jews to disparage their rich cultural and religious heritage but rather to see it through the eyes of a Christian believer. Christian Jews are not obligated to celebrate Passover or any other Jewish feast, either for salvation or sanctification; but if they do observe a feast, it must be to bear witness of what it says about Jesus the Messiah and His gracious work of salvation. We are no longer under the law of Moses.

The epistle to the Hebrews admonishes believers not to miss their inheritance as Israel did at Kadesh Barnea (Numbers 13–14; Hebrews 3–4), but to mature in the faith (Hebrews 5–6) and enjoy the fullness of God's blessing. In their unbelief, Israel wanted to go back to Egypt, and the recipients of the Hebrew epistle wanted to go back to Judaism. The church was being persecuted, and they thought it would be easier just to be devout Jews rather than faithful Christians. How wrong they were! The writer of Hebrews told them not to focus on "religious rituals" on earth—the mere shadows of God's truth—but on the spiritual realities in Christ in heaven (Hebrews 7–10). We must follow the example of Jesus and be willing to suffer as rejects "outside the camp" (Hebrews 13:11–14). We must run the race of faith with endurance and look only to Jesus to help us finish successfully (Hebrews 11–13). To go back to the old life would be to confess that they had never really abandoned it in the first place. Like Israel in the wilderness, these Hebrew believers still had an appetite for the pleasures of Egypt (the world) and failed to serve God wholeheartedly.

This benediction is a rich treasury of some of the spiritual truths found in the Hebrew epistle, truths that can make a difference in our personal lives and in local congregations. The benediction brings together several important elements of the Christian life and applies them to our personal needs and obligations.

COVENANTING—THE FATHER AND THE SON

THE FATHER IS CALLED "the God of peace" and the Son is called "our Lord Jesus," and they work together. The benediction affirms that there is no conflict between the Father and the Son or between

Moses and Jesus. The same God who sent His Son also gave Moses the law, and Jesus affirmed that He came to fulfill the law and not to destroy it (Matthew 5:17–20). Law and grace are not enemies, but partners in the service of God and His people. Law reveals the depth of our depravity and the awesome holiness of God, while grace offers us forgiveness of sins and reconciliation with God. "If you believed Moses, you would believe me," said Jesus, "for he wrote about me" (John 5:46).

What is "the eternal covenant"? It is the covenant made before the foundation of the world by the Father and the Son and the Holy Spirit to work together to save lost sinners. This covenant is intrinsically involved with the new covenant that Jesus established in His blood, the "better covenant" of Hebrews 7:22 and the covenant for which we give thanks when we celebrate the Lord's Supper (Hebrews 8–9).

The Father agreed to call a people and give them to His Son (John 17:2, 6, 9, 11, 24; Acts 15:14). The Son agreed to die for the salvation of sinners and satisfy the justice and holiness of God (Revelation 13:8). He would die for the church (John 10:11; Ephesians 5:25–27), for Israel (Isaiah 53:8); and for the sins of the world (John 3:16). All believers make this truth personal and say with Paul that the Son of God "loved me and gave himself for me" (Galatians 2:20). The Spirit's gift of faith in Jesus (Acts 11:17) brings eternal life to all who believe. You find this cooperative work of the blessed Trinity described in Ephesians 1:3–14 and 1 Peter 1:1–2.

There are mysteries here that we are not able to comprehend, but we can still believe God's Word and join with Paul as he sings, "How unsearchable his judgments and his paths beyond tracing out" (Romans 11:33). We must also keep in mind that God does not want "anyone to perish, but everyone to come to repentance" (2 Peter 3:9) and that He desires "all men to be saved and to come to a knowledge of the truth" (1 Timothy 2:4). Because we can't identify God's elect people from among the lost, we seek to witness to everyone, and we trust the Holy Spirit to call sinners out of darkness and into the light of salvation. For us to do nothing and leave the entire enterprise to God is to grossly misunderstand the Scriptures, for prayer and proclamation are important parts of God's plan to reach the lost (Acts 6:4). The same God who ordains the end—the salvation of sinners—also ordains the means to the end, and we are a part of that means.

CONQVERING—THE EMPTY CROSS AND THE EMPTY TOMB

FAITHFUL TO THE TERMS of the covenant, the Son offered Himself on the cross, willingly dying for the sins of the world. Some people resent a "religion of blood" and oppose it, but the word *blood* is used twenty-one times in the Hebrew epistle, because "without the shedding of blood there is no forgiveness" (Hebrews 9:22). The God of peace made "peace through [Christ's] blood, shed on the cross" (Colossians 1:20; Romans 5:1), and that was the only way peace could have been achieved. "And so Jesus also suffered outside the city gate to make the people holy through his own blood" (Hebrews 13:12). If the religious people who reject the blood of Christ did make it to heaven, they would be miserable, because the slain Lamb is the center of attraction and the inhabitants of heaven sing about His blood (Revelation 5:6–10).

We believe in an empty cross. Jesus is no longer suffering and dying, because "he has appeared once for all at the end of the ages to do away with sin by the sacrifice of himself" (Hebrews 9:26–28; see 7:27). "It is finished!" was His triumphant announcement when He completed His work on the cross, and for anyone to deny that word is to cheapen the cross and the blood that was shed there. In the original Greek text, the form of that cry means, "It is finished, it stands finished, and always will be finished." It was the greatest victory ever won on this earth, for in His sacrifice Jesus conquered sin, Satan, death, and the world system that hates Him.

But the empty cross and the empty tomb go together. The Father kept His covenant promise and "raised him from the dead, freeing him from the agony of death, because it was impossible for death to keep its hold on him" (Acts 2:24; see Psalm 16:8–11). Christ's resurrection was proof that the Father had accepted His sacrifice and that the work of redemption had been completed. "He was delivered over to death for our sins and was raised to life for our justification" (Romans 4:25). The resurrection declares that Jesus is Lord (Acts 2:36) and that His sacrifice on the cross is the only offering the Father will accept for the remission of sins. "And if Christ has not been raised, your faith is futile; you are still in your sins" (1 Corinthians 15:17).

Because Jesus conquered in His death on the cross and His coming forth in glory from the tomb, God's people are "more than conquerors through him" (Romans 8:37). We don't fight *for* victory, but *from* victory, the victory won for us by the suffering, death, and resurrection of Jesus Christ. In Romans 8:38–39, Paul lists the defeated enemies that we no longer need to fear: life and death, Satan's demonic hosts, present circumstances and the unknown future, any powers, anything from heights or the depths—in fact, anything in all of God's creation! The exalted Savior says just about the same thing in Revelation 1:17–18. In his first epistle, John reminds us that believers have overcome the devil (2:13–14), the world (5:4–5), and the false teachers (4:1–4). In the Revelation, John shares Christ's promises to the "overcomers" in the churches (2:7, 11, 17, 26; 3:5, 12, 21; 21:7) and urges them to follow the Lamb because Jesus is the greatest overcomer (17:14).

The cross is empty and the tomb is empty, but God's children share in the fullness of Christ (Colossians 2:9–10) as they draw near to God in full assurance of faith (Hebrews 10:22).

CARING—THE SHEPHERD AND THE FLOCK

MOST SERIOUS BIBLE READERS know that Jesus had a threefold ministry as the shepherd. He is the "good Shepherd" who died for the sheep (John 10:11–18; Psalm 22); the "great Shepherd" who today cares for the sheep (Hebrews 13:20; Psalm 23); and the "Chief Shepherd" who will one day return for His sheep and reward His faithful under-shepherds (1 Peter 5:1–4; Psalm 24). The title *great Shepherd* (literally "the shepherd, the great one") is the equivalent of "great high priest" in Hebrews 4:14 and describes the loving care that Jesus gives to His precious flock that He purchased with His own blood.

I think I was eight years old when I first saw a live sheep. Our third-grade class was taken to a farm where the farmer introduced us not only to the sheep but also to the cows, chickens, horses, and the rest of the farm menagerie. But I already had a good idea of what sheep were like because one Christmas my parents had given me a lovely book all about farm animals. Years later in the Holy Land, my wife and I watched a Jewish shepherd boy skillfully lead his flock and care for them. In Scripture, the flock is one of the major images of the nation of Israel (Numbers 27:17; Isaiah 40:11; Ezekiel 34; Matthew 10:6) as well as one of the church (John 10:1–16; 21:16–17; Acts 20:28). Sinners have gone astray like lost sheep (Isaiah 53:6), but when they turn to Christ by faith, they return "to the Shepherd and Overseer [Bishop] of [their] souls" (1 Peter 2:25).

Some of the greatest men in Old Testament history were shepherds—Abel, Abraham, Isaac, Jacob, Moses, David—but in New Testament times, shepherds did not rank high on the social ladder. Because they lived in the fields with their flocks, shepherds could not worship at the temple or attend the synagogue services; because they constantly handled animals, they were considered unclean. A shepherd was not even permitted to give witness at a trial. Yet Jesus chose to call Himself the Good Shepherd," and the good news of

His birth was given first to shepherds in the fields (Luke 2:1–20). Our English word *pastor* is Latin for "shepherd," and the pastor's calling is to willingly serve and care for the people in the flock and be an example for them to follow (1 Peter 5:1–4).

It's too bad that many people think that Psalm 23 is a Scripture passage only for funerals, because it describes what the exalted High Priest/Shepherd is doing for His people "all the days of [their lives]" (Psalm 23:6). He goes before us and prepares the way. His true sheep recognize His voice (the Word) and follow Him wherever He leads (John 10:4–5). He protects them and feeds them. He calms their fears when they must go through dark dangerous valleys, and at the close of the day, He puts them safely in their fold and guards them all through the night. Nothing in life or death need frighten the sheep because their Shepherd is in complete control. Even in heaven, Jesus Christ will shepherd His people (Revelation 7:17). Meanwhile, let's follow Peter's counsel and cast all our cares on the Good Shepherd, because He cares for us (1 Peter 5:7).

CREATING—THE MASTER ARTIST AND HIS WORK

WE COME NOW to the word *equip*, which is translated "make you perfect [complete]" in the King James Version. To a soldier, the Greek word *katartizo* meant "to equip an army for battle" and to a sailor it meant "to rig a ship for a voyage." In a physician's vocabulary it meant "to set a broken bone," while fishermen used it to mean "to mend the nets" (Matthew 4:21). Teachers used the word to describe students who were "fully trained" (Luke 6:40). The word *katartizo* carries the idea of providing what is needed, repairing what is faulty, and bringing a person or a thing closer to perfection. "Equipped" Christians are adequately prepared for whatever God prepares for them. They are maturing in the Lord and putting away childish things that they might live only for the things that matter most (1 Corinthians 13:11).

The Lord God is the master artist from whom all human artists derive their creativity and skill. If you question that statement, consider the world of nature around you, the galaxies above you, and the remarkable machinery within you. Of course, the atheist or agnostic would give all the credit to "big bangs" and blind chance, but people of faith only smile and say, "We believe in God the Father Almighty, maker of heaven and earth." Though marred, defaced, and even destroyed by the results of Adam's fall and the selfish activities of some of his descendents (Romans 8:20–21), creation still reveals the glorious handiwork of God (Psalm 19; Romans 1:18–20).

But God's most glorious work is the work He is doing with His new creation, the church of Jesus Christ. Today multiplied flaws and defects embarrass the church, but the time will come when she will be "a radiant church, without stain or wrinkle or any other blemish, but holy and blameless" (Ephesians 5:25–27). The Master Artist wants to make us more like Jesus Christ, for in becoming more like Him, we glorify Him by using the abilities and spiritual gifts He has placed within us for the building and beautifying of the church. "It is he who made us, and not we ourselves" (Psalm 100:3 margin). There are no self-made Christians, "for it is God who works in you to will and to act according to his good purpose" (Philippians 2:13). "For we are God's workmanship [*poiema*, or work of art], created in Christ Jesus to do good works, which God prepared in advance for us to do" (Ephesians 2:10).

How does the Lord work in us to transform us into the beautiful image of His Son? How does He equip us for the life He wants to live and the work He wants us to do? Of course, it is the indwelling Spirit of God who accomplishes this miracle ministry, and He cooperates with us as together we use the tools that have been provided.

The Word of God. "All Scripture is inspired by God and profitable for teaching, for reproof, for correction, for training in righteousness; so that the man of God may be adequate [*artios*, 'fit, complete'], equipped [*exartizo*, 'fully furnished and supplied'] for every good work" (2 Timothy 3:16–17 NASB). While secular education is important if we are to minister meaningfully in today's world, it is the heart knowledge of the Word of God that is most important. The believer who reads the Bible faithfully, meditates on it, studies it, memorizes it, and obeys it is the one the Spirit is equipping for service. The Bible instructs us in what is right ("teaching"), what is not right ("reproof"), how to get it right ("correction"), and how to stay right ("training in righteousness"). Once the Scriptures have gripped our own hearts and lives, then we are ready to minister to others; but mere head knowledge will never make us true servants of our Lord.

Prayer. "We are glad whenever we are weak but you are strong; and our prayer is for your perfection [*katartisis*]," Paul wrote to the believers in Corinth (2 Corinthians 13:9). Certainly we ought to be praying for our own balanced equipping in Christian life and service, but we also have the privilege of praying for others. To pray "Bless Joe and Edith" is acceptable, but why not ask the Lord to exercise a *katartizo* ministry on their behalf? Perhaps their ministry tools have been damaged in service and God needs to "mend their nets," or they may be facing an enemy and need equipping for the battle. The Master Artist knows their needs and how to adjust things so they will be at their best.

The Local Church. It's difficult to mature in the Christian life all by ourselves; we need the ministry of others who interact with us to keep us growing and balanced. That's why we need the fellowship of the local church. When the Lord Jesus ascended, He "gave some to be apostles, some to be prophets, some to be evangelists, and some to be pastors and teachers, to prepare [*katartismos*] God's people for works of service, so that the body of Christ may be built up" (Ephesians 4:11–12). No matter what spiritual gift or gifts we may have, each one is needed in the ministry of the local church if the church is to be built up. As we fellowship and serve with God's people, we discover, dedicate, and develop our gifts. This doesn't occur when all we do is listen to a church broadcast or telecast. If we are going to be equipped, we need the interaction of people who know and love us. I thank God for the believers in the church I grew up in. They saw I had a gift for teaching the Word and encouraged me, prayed for me, and gave me opportunities to serve. They also loved me enough to correct me.

Suffering. Nobody enjoys pain, problems, and pressures, but they are an important part of the Christian life. "And the God of all grace, who called you to his eternal glory in Christ, after you have suffered a little while, will himself restore you [*katartizo*] and make you strong, firm and steadfast" (1 Peter 5:10). The people Peter wrote to were experiencing severe suffering (1 Peter 1:6; 2:12, 20; 3:14–17; 4:15), but because they were suffering for the sake of Jesus, their pain was working *for* them and not *against* them. "For our light and momentary troubles are achieving for us an eternal glory that far outweighs them all" (2 Corinthians 4:17), *and the thing that makes the difference is the grace of God.* Of itself, suffering cannot bring spiritual blessing. Instead of making people better, it will make them bitter. But when we trust the God of all grace and draw upon that grace, suffering works for us and brings glory to Jesus Christ. What begins with grace always leads to glory. (We will have more to say about 1 Peter 5:10 in the next chapter).

The Great Shepherd wants to equip us daily "with every good thing for doing his will." He wants to "work in us what is pleasing to him." What joy there is in the family when the children not only obey their parents but also look for other ways to please them without being told. If the blessings of this benediction are working in our lives, then we will be willing to "go to him outside the camp, bearing the disgrace [Jesus] bore" (Hebrews 13:13). The Hebrew believers to whom this letter was addressed wanted to *go back* into the old life when they should have been allowing God to equip them to *go out* into the world to bear witness of Jesus Christ.

That closing phrase—"to whom be glory for ever and ever"—is what spiritual growth is all about.

CHAPTER 16

THE FISHERMAN'S BENEDICTIONS

And the God of all grace, who called you to his eternal glory in Christ, after you have suffered a little while, will himself restore you and make you strong, firm and steadfast. To him be the power for ever and ever. Amen (1 Peter 5:10–11).

But grow in the grace and knowledge of our Lord and Savior Jesus Christ. To him be glory both now and forever! Amen (2 Peter 3:18).

IT GRIEVES ME the way some believers make Simon Peter the target of their feeble jokes. These amateur comedians think they are being clever when really they are being unkind and unlike their Master. Jesus corrected Peter's faults; He didn't magnify them or joke about them.

"You'll know Peter when you get to heaven," these clever people say. "He's the man with the foot-shaped mouth." Or, "Whenever Peter opened his mouth, he changed feet." Or, "Motor-mouth Peter didn't know when to put on the brakes or shift gears."

Shame on them! Not one of them is worthy to carry Peter's sandals let alone ridicule him with such infantile statements. Granted, in the four gospels Peter is finding out what happened to him and what it all meant, and all believers have that experience. But in the book of Acts, Peter certainly lives up to his nickname—the rock. However, if you really want to see what a great man God made out of this common fisherman, read his two epistles.

His first epistle focuses on the grace of God (5:12), and Peter tells us how God's grace helps His people in times of testing and persecution by turning suffering into glory. Peter's theme is "the true grace of God," because there is a false "grace" that leads to easy sinning (Jude 4). In the second letter, Peter deals with spiritual knowledge and how Christians must avoid false teachers by growing in grace and in the knowledge of Jesus Christ (3:17–18). It's obvious that the two benedictions go together, because they emphasize the themes of the two epistles—grace and knowledge. (See John 1:14, 17.) In the first letter, Satan is the lion, bringing suffering to God's people (5:8–9). In the second letter, Satan is the serpent, spreading false doctrine (2:1ff). To defeat the lion we need grace; to defeat the serpent we need spiritual knowledge.

But these two benedictions also remind us of what God wants to do in our lives in times of suffering and trial, and that's where Peter's message of encouragement comes in. These two benedictions reveal at least six exciting truths that bring strength and courage to the people of God in times of trial and testing.

OUR GOD IS ADEQUATE

OUR GOD IS "the God of all grace," and there is no other way to receive grace except to come to the throne of grace and ask for it (Hebrews 4:16). The Bible is "the word of his grace" (Acts 20:32) and tells us what is available, and the Holy Spirit is "the Spirit of grace" (Hebrews 10:29), who applies this grace in our lives. In 1 Peter 4:10, Peter calls it "God's grace in its various forms," but I prefer the Authorized Version's simple "the manifold grace of God." The Greek word translated *manifold* means "many-sided, many-colored." In other words, there is a special grace for every need, every challenge, and every ministry. "Many-colored" reminds us of the rainbow after Noah's flood, the covenant sign that the Lord would never send another judgment like that one. The variety of God's grace matches the variety of the trials ("manifold temptations" in KJV) that come to us in our lives and ministries (1:6).

If you ever begin to doubt the availability and adequacy of divine grace, take time to review the life and ministry of Peter. He was just another Jew when Jesus saved him and promised him he would progress from Simon "the hearer" into Peter "the rock" (John 1:40-42). What a promise Jesus gives him: "You are . . . You will be . . . " (John 1:42). Therefore, never be content with your present condition. As He did with Peter, so Jesus wants to do with us—change us from sand to rock.

Jesus first showed Peter what He could do by using the things that Peter was familiar with in his fishing vocation. He gave him great catches of fish; He calmed storms; He even enabled Peter to walk on the water. Peter caught a fish and found enough money in its mouth to pay the temple tax for himself and for the Lord. Jesus empowered Peter to heal sicknesses and cast out demons, and in the book of Acts, the apostle calmly walked out of a high security prison and went to a prayer meeting. He even raised the dead (Acts 9:40)!

Is the grace of God adequate for every situation? It certainly is! No wonder Peter wrote, "Cast all your anxiety on him because he cares for you" (1 Peter 5:7).

Our God Has Chosen Us

Whenever in the Scriptures you see the word *called* applied to God's people, it's a reminder of God's grace. We can't call on the Lord for salvation until He in His grace first calls us. Christians are people "who are called to belong to Jesus Christ" (Romans 1:6). When Andrew (Peter's brother) brought Peter to Jesus, Peter heard the call to salvation and responded by trusting Christ. Later, he heard Christ's call to discipleship and responded by following Christ (Luke 5:1–11). Paul gives us this wonderful sequence in

Romans 8:28–29. Why would God call sinners like us? It's only because of the super-abounding grace of God.

The experience of "being called" made a lasting impression on Peter, so much so that he used the word often in his letters. In 1 Peter 1:15, he reminds us that we are *called to be holy*. The Christian believer is not to live like the unbelievers in the world (1 Peter 2:11–12), even if it means being persecuted. Christians are to be different. We have also been *"called out of darkness into his wonderful light"* (1 Peter 2:9). This means we walk in the light (1 John 1:5–7) and fellowship with God through His Word. The world prefers to live in the darkness (John 3:19–21), and unless people trust Jesus Christ, they will live in eternal darkness.

In 1 Peter 2:21, we are *called to suffer and follow the example of Christ*. When Jesus was insulted and abused, He did not retaliate but instead trusted the Father to sustain Him and enable Him to return blessing for evil. If our lives are holy and if we are walking in the light, we can be sure we will be attacked by the enemy and persecuted, because that's the way Jesus' enemies treated Him. Paul called this "the fellowship of sharing in his sufferings" (Philippians 3:10). We may not be vindicated and rewarded here on earth, but Peter promises, *"you were called so that you may inherit a blessing"* (1 Peter 3:9). Why be worried about present abuse when we are guaranteed future glory? Furthermore, we receive blessing today even while the enemy attacks us. (See Romans 12:17–21; Matthew 5:11–12.)

This brings us to our benediction in 1 Peter 5:10: we are "called . . . to his eternal glory." In other words, we know we are going to heaven. When Jesus met with His disciples in the upper room—Judas was now absent—He could tell that they were worried and anxious. Twice He told them, "Do not let your hearts be troubled" (John 14:1, 27), *and He reminded them that He would go and prepare a place for them in heaven, the Father's house.* An old gospel song by James M. Grey asked, "And who can mind the journey when the road leads home?" Not only will Jesus give us a glorious home, but He will also give each of His faithful servants a glorious crown (1 Peter 5:4). When we get to heaven, the sufferings we have endured on earth will be insignificant when measured by what Paul calls "an eternal glory that far outweighs them all" (2 Corinthians 4:17).

Instead of trying to solve all the mysteries of God's sovereign electing grace, just bask in the reality of it and the assurance that, come what may, the road leads home.

Our God Is in Control

What begins with God's grace will always lead to God's glory, but between these two experiences we must expect to "suffer a little while." However, we must never permit suffering to weaken our faith or cause us to question God's will or God's love. *We should expect trials and temptations because the Lord told us to expect them.* After all, a faith that can't be tested can't be trusted. You don't become an expert swimmer merely by watching a video or reading a book. You dive into the water! Jesus trained His disciples by putting them into new and difficult experiences and allowing them to learn how weak they were and how strong He was. He follows that same pattern today. There's no growth without challenge and no challenge without change.

In 1 Peter 4:12, Peter compared Christian suffering to a blazing furnace. (The NIV translates it "painful trial," but the original says "a burning, a trial by fire.") Peter had plenty of precedent in the Old Testament for using this metaphor. The sufferings of Israel during their slavery in Egypt are compared to a furnace (Deuteronomy 4:20; 1 Kings 8:51); Job used the same image when describing his intense personal suffering (Job 23:10); and we must not forget the prophet Daniel's three friends in Daniel 3. When we yield to God's will, suffering becomes like a refiner's furnace: it removes the dross and brings out the best.

God knows just when we need a furnace experience: "Even though now for a little while, *if necessary*, you have been distressed by various trials" (1 Peter 1:6 NASB, italics mine). Note that phrase "if necessary." How many times have we prayed, "Lord, is this trial really necessary?" only to have Him answer, "Yes, it is. Trust me." After the disciples had fed over five thousand people, they were feeling important, especially when the people spoke of making Jesus king, so Jesus sent the twelve men into a storm (John 6:15–24). Paul prayed three times that his thorn in the flesh might be removed, but the Lord told him that he needed it (2 Corinthians 12:1–10).

Whenever the Lord puts you into a furnace experience, keep these truths in mind: He knows it is needed, He knows how much is needed, and He knows how long it is needed. Our loving Father keeps His eye on the clock and His hand on the thermostat and is in constant control. Furthermore, He is with us personally in our fiery trials. "So do not fear, for I am with you; do not be dismayed, for I am your God. I will strengthen you and help you; I will uphold you with my righteous right hand" (Isaiah 41:10). King Nebuchadnezzar had three men thrown into the fire, but when he peered into the furnace, he saw four men, and the fourth man looked "like a son of the gods" (Daniel 3:24–25). "And surely I am with you always" (Matthew 28:20).

Our God Is Equipping Us

THE WORD *RESTORE* in this benediction brings back our familiar friend *katartizo*— "equips you, fits you, makes you suitable, adjusts you." The persecuting enemy thinks he is destroying us, but the Lord is using the persecution to equip us and to prepare us for the work and warfare that lies ahead. As we experience "light and momentary trouble," we look forward to a "glory that far outweighs them all" (2 Corinthians 4:17). I emphasized this truth when we studied Hebrews 13:20–21. This benediction is a promise: "And the God of all grace . . . will himself restore you." If we surrender to Him, He will make it happen.

While Moses was taking care of his father-in-law's sheep, the Lord was equipping him to care for a nation of sheep. As Joshua served as Moses' servant, the Lord was fashioning him to be Moses' successor. When young David privately fought and killed a lion and a bear, he was being prepared to defeat a giant publicly. It is indeed a great tragedy for God's people to waste their sufferings and do nothing but complain and argue with the Lord. They are forfeiting their future.

As the Lord equips us, He also enables us ("makes you strong") and establishes us ("make you . . . firm and steadfast"). God puts power within us and a strong foundation beneath us so that we don't fall from weakness or wavering. Believers who are firmly grounded in the faith will not be "blown here and there by every wind of teaching" (Ephesians 4:14) but will stand on the firm foundation of the faith.

Our God Is Maturing Us

This firm foundation is a major theme of Peter's second letter in which he affirms the truth of the apostolic message and admonishes his readers to make their "calling and election sure" (1:10–21). He describes the false teachers who were denying the promise of the Lord's return (chapters 2 and 3) and then closes with a warning against listening to false doctrine lest they be "carried away by the error of lawless men and fall from [their] secure position" (2 Peter 3:17). The solution? "But grow in the grace and knowledge of our Lord and Savior Jesus Christ" (2 Peter 3:18).

There is a difference between age and maturity. The fact that people have lived for fifty years is no guarantee they are mature in their thinking or their living. Growing old and "growing up" are two vastly different processes. When little children learn to walk, they think they can imitate their older siblings and run everywhere and do everything, but this often leads to bruises and broken bones. As children mature, they eventually develop their motor skills and graduate to bicycles, then roller blades, then to skateboards, and then to automobiles and motorcycles. But the ability to stand firmly is the basis for whatever they do with their feet.

To grow in the grace of Jesus Christ has to do with our character and conduct, a blessing that accompanies growing in the knowledge of Jesus Christ. Peter was refuting the false teachers of that day by emphasizing the importance of true spiritual knowledge. To get to know Jesus Christ better day by day is to grow to be more like Him day by day (Ephesians 4:13–16). But I must issue a caution here: it is easier to grow in Bible knowledge and get a "big head" than it is to assimilate this truth and grow in grace. "Knowledge puffs up, but love builds up" (1 Corinthians 8:1). All of us have met Christians who know their Bibles well but don't practice what the Bible commands. Even Satan can quote the Bible (Matthew 4:5–7).

We are not to be cute little saplings but mature trees that bear fruit (Psalm 1:3). We may begin as lambs, but we must grow to become productive sheep. First John 2:12–14 suggests stages in spiritual growth, from little children to young people to fathers. Hebrews 5:11–14 describes believers who had been saved long enough to become teachers, but instead they were in a "second childhood" and had to learn the basics all over. The milk of the Word is the truth involved in what Jesus did on earth—His birth, life and ministry, death and resurrection. But the meat of the Word (the solid food, 1 Corinthians 3:1–3) is the truth about what He is doing for us today in heaven as our High Priest. The present heavenly ministry of Christ is one of the important themes of Hebrews.

Christians grow from the inside out. God's truth must penetrate our hearts, be "digested," and become a part of our inner being, or it will do us little good. Christians grow best in a family setting, and that's where the local church comes in. We need the encouragement of other believers as well as their prayers, warnings, and counsel. "All the believers were together," Luke wrote of the first Christian congregation (Acts 2:44), a good example for us to follow today. They heard the Word together, prayed together, and ate together, and when they scattered, they shared the good news of Jesus Christ.

God's grace doesn't grow; *we* grow in our knowledge and understanding of His grace and in our appropriation of that grace as we have need. The more we learn about Jesus Christ, the more we realize the spiritual treasures God has made available through Christ. "From the fullness of his grace we have all received one blessing after another" (John 1:16). The image in that verse is of ocean waves coming onto shore, one after the other in endless fullness. We are like little children on the beach, trying to capture the ocean in our little pails. "But he gives us more grace," says James 4:6. "That is why the Scripture says: 'God opposes the proud but gives grace to the humble.'"

> O to grace how great a debtor
> Daily I'm constrained to be!
> Let Thy goodness, like a fetter,
> Bind my wandering heart to Thee.
>
> —Robert Robinson

OUR GOD RECEIVES THE GLORY

"To HIM BE THE GLORY both now and forever. Amen." Once again we see that whatever begins with God's grace ends with God's glory. It has well been said that there is nothing God will not do for those who let Him alone have the glory. "I am the Lord; that is my name! I will not give my glory to another or my praise to idols" (Isaiah 42:8). Whatever glory famous men and women have in this world will not last, but the glory of the Lord will last forever; and any servants of God who take the glory to themselves will regret it when they see the Lord.

When evangelist D. L. Moody was preaching in Birmingham, England, the well-known preacher of that city, R. W. Dale, reported that he told Moody that "the work was plainly of God, for I could see no real relation between him and what he had done. [Moody] laughed cheerily, and said he should be very sorry if it were otherwise" (*The Life of R. W. Dale of Birmingham,* 318). This reminds us of the great desire that motivated John the Baptist: "He [Jesus] must become greater; I must become less" (John 3:30).

Thank you, Peter, for teaching us so much about Jesus and what He wants to do in our lives.

CHAPTER 17

THE JOYFUL BENEDICTION

To him who is able to keep you from falling and to present you before his glorious presence without fault and with great joy—to the only God our Savior be glory, majesty, power and authority, through Jesus Christ our Lord, before all ages, now and forevermore! Amen (Jude 24–25).

THE NAME JUDE is short for Judah ("praise" in the Hebrew), and this particular Jude was a half-brother of our Lord Jesus Christ (Matthew 13:55; Mark 6:3). However, being a humble man, he identified himself as "a brother of James," who was an early leader of the Jerusalem church (Acts 12:17; 15:13; Galatians 1:19) and the author of the epistle of James (James 1:1). Neither Jude nor James had trusted Christ until after our Lord's resurrection (John 7:1–5; 1 Corinthians 15:7), and then they identified with the church in Jerusalem (Acts 1:12–14).

Jude started to write a letter about "the salvation we share" (v. 3) but was led by the Spirit to focus on the dangerous unsaved people in the church (v. 19) who were teaching false doctrine and turning "the grace of our God into a license for immorality" (v. 4). Both Paul and Peter also warned about this deadly menace (Acts 20:27–31; 2 Peter 2). Using a number of vivid metaphors, Jude described these false teachers and pronounced their ultimate doom (vv. 5–16). He closed his brief letter by telling the true believers how to remain faithful (vv. 17–23) and then added this beautiful benediction with its promise of security, eternal glory, and joy.

When we read this letter carefully, we discover that among the warnings, Jude added an emphasis on love (vv. 1, 2, 12, and 21).

In fact, three times he addressed his readers as "beloved" (3, 17, 20; "dear friends" in the NIV). Along with love, there is also an emphasis on being kept or guarded (vv. 1, 21, and 24). Though others may masquerade as believers and pollute the church, we can be faithful to the Lord and build the church and our lives in holiness.

In his benediction, Jude mentions three tenses: "before all ages, now and forevermore" (v. 25), and these three tenses parallel Jude's three statements about "keeping."

"Before all ages"—We were kept *for* Jesus (v. 1)
"Now"—We are kept (guarded) *by* Jesus (v. 24a)
"Forevermore"—We shall be kept *with* Jesus (v. 24b)

Jude's letter is indeed a needed word of warning, but woven into its texture is a message to God's people of love and security and the promise of a glorious future. Only those who are counterfeits, who "do not have the Spirit" (v. 19), need to be afraid.

"BEFORE ALL AGES"—KEPT *FOR* JESUS (vv. 1–2)

THE GREEK PREPOSITION *ev* can be translated "for," "by" or "in," and all three translations are valid. We are kept *in* Jesus and *by* Jesus, but I prefer to translate the phrase "kept *for* Jesus Christ," because that translation fits best with the other "kept" verses in Jude. We begin with eternity past, then we come to the present age, and then we move into eternity future.

You will recall when we studied the shepherd benediction (Hebrews 13:20–21) that we learned about an eternal covenant the Father and the Son and the Holy Spirit made for the salvation of lost sinners. This covenant is summarized in Ephesians 1:3–14. The Father chose a people to become the bride of His Son (Ephesians 1:3–6); the Son died to save them (Ephesians 1:7–12); and the Holy Spirit applied that salvation to their lives and sealed them as His own for eternity (Ephesians 1:13–14). All of this was for the praise of God's glory and grace.

There are many mysteries about God's plan of salvation, but one thing is obvious: the whole Godhead is involved. The Father has chosen us, but we knew nothing about that until after we entered the family of God and studied His Word. Jesus died for us, and it was that message that we believed and by which we were saved; and then the Spirit sealed the transaction for all eternity. It takes all three. Salvation doesn't start with us; it starts with the Father's sovereign choice in eternity past. "Salvation comes from the Lord" (Jonah 2:9). It is a gift of His grace. Salvation by works and character would inflate the ego, but salvation wholly by sovereign grace humbles us and moves us to praise the Lord.

The doctors told my mother that I probably wouldn't live past the age of two, but God had other plans. My great-grandfather (whom I never knew) often prayed that there would be a preacher of the gospel in every generation of our family, and there has been. The Lord had chosen me to be that preacher in my generation. Of course, as a child I knew nothing about that; but the Lord watched over me and "kept me for Jesus Christ." Before there ever was a universe, as we know it, the Lord was thinking about me and planning for me. When I think about this, it overwhelms me with gratitude and makes me ask, "Why me, Lord?"

The Father grants eternal life to all those He has chosen and given to Jesus (John 17:2). We don't know who they are until they trust the Lord, so we share the gospel with as many as we can, knowing that Jesus died for the sins of the world (1 John 2:2; 4:14). Note in John 17 that Jesus often refers to His people as the Father's gift to Him (vv. 2, 6, 9, 24). Jesus is the Father's gift to us (John 3:16), and we are the Father's gift to His Son. Wonder of wonders!

Whenever a sinner trusts Jesus and is born again, we have to believe in the sovereign grace and providence of God. Why didn't I die at the age of two? Why did I attend that Youth for Christ rally at the high school auditorium? Why did Billy Graham's message convict my heart that night? After all, I had attended Sunday school since childhood and was confirmed in the church. Why? Because God loved me and kept me for His Son, and then He called me that night out of darkness into the light of salvation. I received the gift of salvation, and the Father made me His gift to His Son. Amazing grace!

Please don't get lost in the labyrinth of theological arguments about divine sovereignty and human responsibility. The greatest question isn't, "How do we reconcile the two?" The greatest question is, "Why did He choose us?" Let's just imitate Paul and fall before the Lord and worship Him. "Oh, the depth of the riches of the wisdom and knowledge of God! How unsearchable his judgments, and his paths beyond tracing out" (Romans 11:33)!

"Ποω"—Κεpτ by Jesus (24a)

AFTER DESCRIBING THE godless apostates in verses 4–19, Jude addressed the true believers in a rather abrupt fashion—"But you, beloved" (v. 20). In other words, "The Lord expects you to be different!" After all, these believers had been loved by God the Father and kept for Jesus Christ, and they had experienced God's mercy, peace, and love. Jude assured his readers that the Lord was not only able to keep them from falling but even from stumbling, which is the preferred translation of *aptaistos*. Of course, stumbling may easily lead to falling, but those who have made their "calling and election sure . . . will never fall," even if they do stumble (2 Peter 1:10–11).

Jude gave his readers clear instructions for walking safely, starting with *remembering the Word of God* (vv. 17–19). The Scriptures give us the light that we need (Psalm 119:9–11, 105), and as we obey God's will, the way before us becomes clearer. We walk a step at a time, and there is always enough light for us to see where to put the next step. The Lord guards His people as they walk in the light of His will (John 11:9–10; 1 John 1:5–10). We avoid the dangerous detours by staying on His level path (Proverbs 4:10–19). Whenever we go our own way and trust in our own wisdom, we tempt the Lord and are in danger of stumbling (Proverbs 3:5–6). Jude's next admonition is to *keep building our faith* (v. 20a). Paul calls this "edification" (Romans 14:19; 1 Corinthians 14:4–5, 17; and note Acts 20:32). This means growing in grace and in the knowledge of Jesus as revealed in the Word (2 Peter 3:18), spending time in fellowship with God's people, and training ourselves in godliness (1 Timothy 4:7–8). *Praying in the Holy Spirit* (20b) accompanies studying the Scriptures, because the Word and prayer go together and bring balance to our lives (1 Samuel 12:23; John 15:7; Acts 6:4). All Bible and no prayer means "light without heat," and all prayer without the Bible means "zeal without knowledge." The Holy Spirit uses the Scriptures to direct us and correct us in our praying so that we learn to pray in the will of God (Romans 8:26).

When we obey "Keep yourselves in God's love" (v. 21), we cooperate with the Lord so that He can keep us from stumbling. "Whoever has my commands and obeys them, he is the one who loves me. He who loves me will be loved by my Father, and I too will love him and show myself to him" (John 14:21). God's love for us is unchanging, but we cannot experience His love if we are careless and disobedient (2 Corinthians 6:14–18). Like the church at Ephesus, we may leave our first love and grow careless (Revelation 2:4). God cannot be a Father to us if we are rebellious children. Some people speak of God's "unconditional love" as though the Father has no standards for His children and tolerates their disobedience with a smile. They need to read Hebrews 12 and learn that God shows His love in His disciplines as well as in His delights. Ponder God's dealings with King David after his sin with Bathsheba and his murder of her husband. As Spurgeon said, "God will not permit His children to sin successfully."

A powerful antidote to temptation and disobedience is *looking for the return of the Lord* (v. 21). "Everyone who has this hope in him purifies himself, just as he is pure" (1 John 3:3). In a number of His parables, Jesus commands us to "watch" and "be ready" for the return of the Lord (Matthew 24:36–51; Luke 17:20–37). While we are waiting, we should also be serving (vv. 22–23), and while helping others we must be careful not to get soiled ourselves (see James 1:27). In our zeal to win the lost, we must exercise discernment lest we become contaminated ourselves.

Our part in ministry is to obey God's commands (vv. 17–23), and God's part is to provide the wisdom and strength that keeps us faithful (vv. 24–25). He is able to keep us from stumbling because we keep ourselves in His love and prove that love by our obedience. God is able to make us stand (Romans 14:4), so why should we stumble?

"FOREVERMORE"—KEPT *with* JESUS (24B–25)

JESUS IS PREPARING a home in heaven for His people (John 14:1–6). With that home, He is preparing an inheritance "that can never perish, spoil or fade" because it is "kept in heaven for you, who through faith are shielded by God's power" (1 Peter 1:4–5). The time is coming when the church will stand in the presence of God and share in the glory that Jesus prayed about before He went to the cross (John 17:22–24). *We shall see His glory and share His glory!* We shall also share His likeness (1 John 3:1–2, Philippians 3:20–21). What a day that will be!

> Hallelujah!
>   For our Lord God almighty reigns!
> Let us rejoice and be glad and give him glory!
> For the wedding of the Lamb has come,
>   and his bride has made herself ready (Revelation 19:6–
>   7).

I have performed many marriages, knowing full well that nobody was paying much attention to the preacher or the bridegroom, for the congregation's attention was on the bride. The church was "kept *for* Jesus Christ"—that was the engagement; kept *by* Jesus Christ during her earthly pilgrimage; and one day the church will be married to the beloved Bridegroom and will be kept *with* Jesus for eternity! "Blessed are those who are invited to the wedding supper of the Lamb! (Revelation 19:9).

Today, the church is stained, wrinkled, and blemished (Ephesians 5:27), but when we stand before the throne of the Father ("God our Savior"—Psalm 42:5, 11; Isaiah 17:10; Habakkuk 3:18; Luke 1:47; 1 Timothy 1:1), we will be "without fault" and "blameless." When the Son presents His bride to His Father, there will be nothing unacceptable to the Father, for the bride will be "holy and blameless" (Ephesians 5:27). The marriage of the Lamb will be an occasion of exceedingly great joy. Just anticipating this event ought to make us love Him more and want to serve Him better.

Yes, God's people will be kept with Jesus forevermore. We don't deserve this matchless gift, but it is ours because we belong to Jesus Christ. God will keep us in His love, but those without Christ will be kept in "blackest darkness . . . reserved forever" (Jude 13).

Ruth Bell Graham has put this benediction into a beautiful poem that can be used to close a service of worship.

Now unto Him Who is able
spotless to keep His own,
presenting each ransomed sinner
blameless before the throne,
to the only wise God, our Father,
to Him Whom we all adore,
be glory, dominion, and power
both now and forevermore.[10]

CHAPTER 18

THE BENEDICTION OF THE BLOOD

To him who loves us and has freed us from our sins by his blood, and has made us to be a kingdom and priests to serve his God and Father—to him be glory and power for ever and ever! Amen (Revelation 1:5b–6).

THE APOSTLE JOHN was a prisoner of Rome on the island of Patmos in the Aegean Sea, some fifty miles from the believers in Ephesus where he had ministered. The Roman government wanted citizens to say "Caesar is Lord!" but Christians responded with "Jesus is Lord!" This Caesar would not accept.

One Lord's Day, John received from the Lord—and wrote down—a series of visions that we call the book of Revelation, the last book in the Bible. While this book is a prophecy (Revelation 1:3, 22:7, 10, 18, 19), it is also "the testimony of Jesus Christ" (1:2). It is not only a revelation of future events but also primarily a revelation of the Son of God who controls those events. John recorded in chapter one the vision he had of his Lord, the ascended and glorified King-Priest, but he also saw Jesus as the slain Lamb (chapter 5) and the victorious Conqueror (chapter 19). Scattered throughout the book you see "glimpses" of Jesus, and you hear His voice speaking to His people. He speaks to the churches in chapters 2 and 3 and seven times commands us to pay attention to what is said to each church.

It is important to see the plural pronoun *us* in this benediction. John wrote the book for all believers in the churches, and we can claim for ourselves the blessings that he shares. This is the only book in the Bible that specifically promises a blessing to those who read it, hear it, and take it to heart (1:3). The fact that Jesus sent this book to churches (plural) shows the importance of the local church in the plan of God. There are all kinds of religious organizations, many of them doing excellent work, but the local church must take precedence over them all.

The benediction speaks of three precious gifts, two that Jesus gives to us, and one that we should give to Him.

LOVE—JESUS GIVES HIMSELF *TO* US

THE TENSE OF THE VERB is important—He "*loves* us." Today. Now. John was an exile, but he was still experiencing the love of Jesus in the midst of his suffering. Remember, John was called "the disciple whom Jesus loved" (John 13:23; 19:26; 20:2; 21:7, 20), and that love didn't end when Jesus returned to heaven. In the upper room, John heard Jesus say, "Whoever has my commands and obeys them, he is the one who loves me. He who loves me will be loved by my Father, and I too will love him and show myself to him" (John 14:21). John loved Jesus, and Jesus revealed Himself to him. We will not see the dramatic visions that John saw and wrote about, but the Spirit can open "the eyes of [our] heart" (Ephesians 1:18) to see Jesus in the Word, and we will worship him.

Love means giving ourselves to others, and because Jesus loves us, He is constantly giving of Himself to us by the Spirit through the Word. When we love people, we give them our time, resources, encouragement, and help, and we sacrifice gladly. That is the way love operates.

But note John's posture: when he saw the glorified Christ, he "fell at His feet as though dead" (Revelation 1:17). In the upper room, John had leaned on Jesus' breast (John 13:21–27; 21:20), but now he fell at His feet. To use the words of Paul, John was no longer regarding Jesus "from a worldly point of view"

(2 Corinthians 5:16). Since Christ's resurrection and ascension and the coming of the Holy Spirit, the glorified Savior relates to us in a deeper and more spiritual way than He did to His disciples while on earth. They heard Him, saw Him, studied Him, and even felt Him (1 John 1:1), but since His ascension, believers apprehend Jesus through the Spirit teaching the Word. Jesus today is in a glorified body; therefore, He is not limited by time or space but is always available to His people everywhere. We must go beyond the babe in the manger and the gentle carpenter and worship the glorified Son of God.

In public prayer, worship, and ministry, God's people must avoid expressing a kind of familiarity and "chumminess" that is unbiblical. How we fellowship with the Lord in private is one thing, but in public we must seek to glorify Jesus and edify the church. In Revelation 1:5, John called his Lord "the faithful witness" (Prophet and word), "the firstborn[11] from the dead" (Priest and sacrifice), "and the ruler of the kings of the earth" (King of kings), titles that ought to humble us and put us at His feet. If John, who knew Him so well, was "slain" by the vision of the glorified Christ, where does that leave us who live centuries later?

When he wrote his gospel, John used the word *love* (noun and verb) over sixty times. In John 11, three times John tells us that Jesus loved Mary, Martha, and Lazarus (John 11:3, 5, 36), *and yet He permitted Lazarus to become ill, get worse, and die!* Instead of rushing to the home of His beloved friends, Jesus tarried two days. Yes, bad things can happen to people whom Jesus loves, and sometimes Jesus even shows His love by delaying instead of acting immediately. We must never judge God's love by the circumstances of life. No matter what He allows to happen to us, He still loves us and will be glorified in the end. The children's hymn says it perfectly:

Jesus loves me! This I know,
For the Bible tells me so.

—Anna B. Warner

FREEDOM—JESUS GAVE HIMSELF FOR US

SOME TRANSLATIONS READ "washed us from our sins," which is certainly a valid statement (Revelation 7:14; 1 John 1:7; Hebrews 9:14), but the preferred translation is "freed." If love is a major theme in John's gospel, then victory over sin is a major theme of his first epistle. "My dear children, I write this to you so that you will not sin" (1 John 1:5–10; 2:1; 4:1–6; 5:1–5). "You dear children, are from God and have overcome them [the false teachers], because the one who is in you is greater than the one who is in the world" (1 John 4:4). That refers to the Holy Spirit.

Jesus is our Redeemer, and the price He paid for our ransom was His own life, his blood given on the cross (Matthew 20:28). Our forgiveness is because of His blood (Ephesians 1:7; Colossians 1:14), and we are delivered from the curse of the law by His blood (Galatians 3:13). We were set free from our "empty way of life," not by silver and gold but "with the precious blood of Christ" (1 Peter 1:18–19). The redemption we have is eternal (Hebrews 9:12), and one day our bodies will also be redeemed and we shall be like Jesus (Romans 8:23; Ephesians 1:14; 1 John 3:1–2). As the theologians express it, because Jesus gave His blood for us, we have been liberated from the penalty of sin, we are being saved from the power of sin, and, when He returns, we shall be saved from the presence of sin.

When Old Testament Jews thought of redemption, they would probably remember the exodus of Israel from Egypt. The Jews were saved from death by the shedding and applying of the blood of the lamb, and they were saved from bondage by the opening of the Red Sea. These two events picture what Jesus has done for His church: as our Passover Lamb, He shed His blood for us (1 Corinthians 5:7–8), and He came forth from the tomb to ascend to heaven, where we are now seated with Him (Ephesians 2:6). He opened the way for us! It's also worth noting that it was God's love for Israel that motivated these wonderful acts (Deuteronomy 4:37; 7:7–8; 23:5), just as Christ's love for us motivated Him to die for us on the cross (Romans 5:8; John 15:12–13).

It's tragic that the nation of Israel often wanted to abandon their freedom and return to Egypt. They found it difficult to live by faith and trust God to meet their needs as they made their way through the wilderness to the Promised Land. But are believers today any different? How often God's children are tempted to question His promises and His providence and go back into the world! We must walk by faith and not by sight (2 Corinthians 5:7), because it is only by faith and patience that we can claim His promises (Hebrews 6:12). "It is for freedom that Christ has set us free. Stand firm, then, and do not let yourselves be burdened again by a yoke of slavery" (Galatians 5:1). Paul was referring to the yoke of the Mosaic law (Acts 15:10), from which Jesus has delivered us (Romans 6:14–15).

Our freedom is expensive, for it demanded the blood of Jesus; therefore, we must not go back into the bondage of the world, the flesh (Romans 6), or the devil. However, our freedom is not license to sin, nor does our deliverance from the law make us lawless (Galatians 5:13–15). Freedom means life motivated by love and controlled by truth, for the truth sets us free (John 8:31–32). Whenever we are motivated by hatred and selfishness and controlled by lies, we are in bondage, no matter how free we may feel. Our greatest bondage is to have our own way; our greatest freedom is to let God have His way. He always gives His best to those who leave the choice with Him.

SERVICE—WE GIVE OURSELVES TO HIM

THE LORD JESUS Christ has "made us . . . to serve." "For we are God's workmanship, created in Christ Jesus to good works, which God prepared in advance for us to do" (Ephesians 2:10). God knows what He wants us to do, and through the Holy Spirit He has given us the gifts and power we need to accomplish His work.

We are no longer slaves to sin but slaves to righteousness and to God (Romans 6:6, 16–22), and it is as God's slaves we enjoy true freedom.

Note the two metaphors John used: collectively, God's people are a kingdom and a holy priesthood (Revelation 5:10; see 1 Peter 2:5, 9). In John's day, the Roman Empire was the ruling kingdom, and an awesome kingdom it was. It is pictured as the iron legs of the great image in Daniel 2 and as the terrifying beast in Daniel 7. But scattered throughout the Roman Empire was a powerful kingdom that would endure long after Rome had crumbled—the kingdom of God on earth. John pictured the kingdom of this world as a corrupt and wealthy city, Babylon the Great (Revelation 17–18), and in every age there has been a manifestation of Babylon. But one day the kingdom of this world will become "the kingdom of our Lord and of his Christ, and he will reign for ever and ever" (Revelation 11:15).

The combination of kings and priests is unique because the Jews kept the two offices separated. King Uzziah tried to invade the temple and burn incense, and the Lord struck him with leprosy (2 Chronicles 26:16–23). The only king-priest we find in the Old Testament is Melchizedek, who met Abraham and blessed him (Genesis 14). The Scriptures promised that a Redeemer would come and minister as both king and priest, and in Him the temple and the throne would be united (Psalm 110:4; Zechariah 6:13). That Redeemer, of course, is Jesus Christ, who today serves in heaven as a "priest forever in the order of Melchizedek" (Hebrews 6:13–7:28). He is both King and Priest, and the people of God serve with Him today as kings and priests. As kings, we shall reign with Him for a thousand years on the earth (Revelation 3:21; 5:10; 20:4, 6) and forever in heaven (Revelation 22:5).

The fact that in Jesus Christ we are kings should encourage us to live like kings. We have the authority of His name (Acts 3:6, 16; 4:10–12; Philippians 2:1–10), we can come boldly to His throne of grace (Hebrews 4:14–16), and we have access to His wealth (Romans 11:33; Ephesians 1:7; Philippians 4:19). When as a teenager I was confirmed in the church, our confirmation hymn was "A Child of the King" by Harriet E. Buell. I have not heard the song sung or even mentioned for years, but its message is still meaningful to me.

> My Father is rich in houses and lands,
> He holdeth the wealth of the world in his hands!
> Of rubies and diamonds, of silver and gold,
> His coffers are full, He has riches untold.
> I'm a child of the King, a child of the King,
> With Jesus, my Savior, I'm a child of the King.

Peter calls believers "a royal priesthood" (1 Peter 2:9), which again links us to the king-priest Melchizedek, and in 1 Peter 2:5, Peter informs us that as priests we have the privilege of offering "spiritual sacrifices" to the Lord through Jesus Christ. The word *spiritual* is used in contrast to the ceremonial sacrifices the priests offered under the old covenant that were only types and shadows of what was to come. Our sacrifices take on a spiritual quality because they are offered through our High Priest Jesus Christ, as the Holy Spirit in our hearts helps us offer them to God's glory. Let me list a few of these "spiritual sacrifices."

- the body of the believer (Romans 12:1–2)
- the believer's humble broken heart (Psalm 51:17)
- believing prayer from the heart (Psalm 141:2)
- sincere praise (Hebrews 13:15)
- good works in Jesus' name (Hebrews 13:16)
- material possessions, including money (Philippians 4:14–19)
- people we lead to faith in Christ (Romans 15:16)

The believer's body is a living sacrifice, which means that everything we do with our body in daily life is offered to the Lord for His glory (1 Corinthians 6:19–20). When we are at worship, we must praise the Lord the best we can, because praise is a sacrifice for His glory. Praise must be energized by the Spirit of God and founded on the Word of God (Ephesians 5:18–20; Colossians 3:16). Go through that brief list of spiritual sacrifices, look up the texts and read them, and note that the condition of the heart is the important thing. Then read 1 Samuel 15. "Man looks at the outward appearance, but the Lord looks at the heart" (1 Samuel 16:7).

When John was among the apostles during our Lord's days on earth, he and his brother James persuaded their mother to ask Jesus to give each of them a special throne at His side in the kingdom. This request angered the other apostles and grieved the Lord. (See Matthew 20:20–28.) Jesus promised the apostles that they would sit on the thrones in the kingdom, but He warned James and John that they didn't know what they were asking for. *We shouldn't ask for rewards, because we must earn them; and we don't desire them for our praise, but for the glory of Jesus Christ.* "If we endure, we will also reign with him" (2 Timothy 2:12), and that means we must suffer.

Moment by moment, Jesus is giving Himself *to* us, and in the past He gave Himself *for* us. Our logical response is to give ourselves to Him and serve Him and the Father in the power of the Spirit. We are a priestly kingdom. Let's live like it!

———

WHEN JOHN WROTE this benediction, it must have meant much to him because it perfectly fit his situation at that hour. The Romans had arrested him and exiled him, yet he belonged to a kingdom that would never end. Daniel's prophecies were fulfilled, and the Roman Empire passed off the scene, but the kingdom of Jesus still stands.

John was experiencing hatred and severe official persecution, yet he had the love of Jesus in his heart, and nobody could take that away. He was isolated from his beloved friends in the church at Ephesus, but as priests of God, they could pray for one another.

Physically, John was a prisoner being told what to do; but in his heart, he was a free man because of the blood of Jesus Christ. His heart was free to worship the Lord. His mind was free to think of the Lord and meditate on the Scriptures he knew so well.

And John ministered to the saints of that time and would minister to saints in every generation that followed, including God's people today. Doors were closed to him on earth, but God in His grace opened the doors of heaven and allowed John to hear and see remarkable things and then communicate them to us. (Paul went to heaven, but when he came back, he wasn't permitted to tell us what he heard.) Ministry isn't determined by our circumstances on earth but by our resources from heaven.

To Jesus Christ be glory and power forever and ever!

Will you say amen to that?

CHAPTER 19

BE A BLESSING!

"... I will bless you ... and you will be a blessing" (Genesis 12:2).

WHAT THE LORD said to Abraham centuries ago, He is saying to all of His children today: "Trust me and obey me and I will bless you, and you will be a blessing."

It is a wonderful thing to *receive* a blessing, but it is even more wonderful to *be* a blessing. Our world needs benediction Christians.

You do not need to take a seminary course or learn to read Greek or Hebrew in order to be a blessing to others. Christians are not supposed to be reservoirs for the storing and protecting of blessings. We are to be channels for the sharing of our blessings. Most of us are praying, "Lord, give me a blessing" when we ought to be praying, "Lord, make me a blessing."

God kept His promise to Abraham, or I would not be writing this book. Everything in my life that is precious came to me from Abraham and the Jewish people: the knowledge of the one true and living God, the written Word of God, and the Son of God who is my Lord and Savior. Abraham and his people have been a great blessing to me, and I have tried to be a blessing to others as the Lord has enabled me.

I'm grateful for the church of my childhood and youth, for the prayers of the people, and the opportunities they gave me to learn and to serve. If believers cannot be a blessing in their own home church, how can they be a blessing out on the battlefield of this world? I confess that I am a little afraid of the "solitary saints" who ignore the church and found their own organizations so they can "serve the Lord." Let's begin where the New Testament believers began—serving in the local church first. Get your blessings there, and share your blessings there.

Every local church should be a blessing to the people who attend. Regular Bible study, worship, prayer, and fellowship are vitally important to the "benediction believer." As I have said elsewhere, we belong to each other, we affect each other, and we need each other. The solitary saint is too often out of balance spiritually. We need other Christians so we can synchronize our watches and be sure our compasses are in working order. Iron sharpens iron, and we can get pretty dull fellowshiping only with ourselves. Too many saints are walking down lover's lane by themselves, holding their own hand. They need other people.

I suggest that every church service begin with an invocation, a biblical prayer to the Lord that expresses our heart's desire for Him to come to the assembly and bless the brothers and sisters who have met to worship. "Oh, that you would rend the heavens and come down, that the mountains would tremble before you!" (Isaiah 64:1). Sunday services must not become "business as usual." Let's plead for the showers of blessing.

I like to hear a benediction at the close of the meeting so that I can leave the sanctuary with the assurance that the same Lord who came to bless our meeting is going with us as we depart. We want Him to make us a blessing to others in the days that follow. After successfully bringing the ark of the covenant to Jerusalem, David went home to bless his household and discovered that his wife Michal really needed a blessing. David reacted to her criticism instead of responding to her needs, and the blessing never came (see 2 Samuel 6). Charity starts at home, and so does sharing God's blessing.

In recent years, worship has become too casual in many churches. There is usually no invocation but only a welcome from a worship team member as he or she smiles and strums a guitar.

And there is usually no planned benediction. Sometimes there is a closing prayer that either summarizes the sermon or repeats the important announcements, but such things do not send us forth fortified by the blessing of God. "Thanks for worshiping with us," we hear. "You are dismissed." How much better it would be if we were dismissed with a biblical benediction that could lodge in our hearts, grow, and encourage us the rest of the week.

So if you want to be a blessing, start right at home, in your own family and in your own church family. If a move to be more contemporary has omitted the invocation and benediction from your worship service, pray about it and talk with the pastor. Be patient and prayerful and ask God to work in His way. It is time our churches started catching up on the past.

Have you ever noticed that the believer in Psalm 1 who received a blessing in verses 1 and 2 *became* a blessing in verse 3?

> Blessed is the man
> who does not walk in the counsel of the wicked
> or stand in the way of sinners
> or sit in the seat of mockers.
> But his delight is in the law of the Lord,
> and on his law he meditates day and night.
> He is like a tree planted by streams of water,
> which yields its fruit in season
> and whose leaf does not wither.
> Whatever he does prospers.

In the first two verses, he was obeying God's Word in his everyday life (walking, standing, sitting) and meditating faithfully on the Word day and night. In time, he became like a tree—rooted in the soil, taking in the water from the river (the Holy Spirit, John 7:37), and producing shade and fruit *for others to enjoy.* The tree does not eat the fruit. The fruit is for the hungry people who need a blessing from God.

It is obvious that we cannot give to others what we do not possess ourselves. "Silver or gold I do not have," Peter told the crippled beggar, "but what I have I give you" (Acts 3:6). What Peter had was just what the man needed. This is a good example for us to follow each day as we set out to work, school, or whatever we do. Whether like Peter and John we are going to a prayer meeting or like Paul touring the city of Athens (Acts 17) or like Jesus sitting at a well needing a drink of water (John 4), we can share what the Lord has given us and bring blessing to others. Yes, it takes spiritual discernment to know just how to approach people, but the Lord gives us that as we step out by faith. If we begin each day asking the Lord to make us a blessing to others, He will providentially arrange our steps—and stops—and lead us to the people who need God's blessing.

My wife and I drove to our local airport to turn some mileage points into a ticket for a friend. I asked an employee if our friend Harry (not his real name) was still working there, and sure enough, there he was, talking on the phone. Because my wife and I were no longer traveling in a ministry, we had not seen him for several years. As we conversed, we discovered he was facing some serious personal problems, so we tarried to encourage him and pray with him, and we took the burden home for continued intercession. Had we shown up a few minutes later, we might have missed him. If you want to be a blessing, God will make it happen. In the life of the benediction believer, there are no accidents—only appointments. If we are prepared to bless, God is prepared to work.

But being a blessing involves not just personal contacts and conversations; you can share God's blessings over the telephone, by e-mail or fax, by writing a personal letter, even by sending a book or a copy of an article. Some years ago, the enemy was attacking our ministry and us in a serious way, and I was at low ebb. The phone rang, and it was a Christian friend with whom I had occasionally served in conference ministry.

"The Lord told me to phone you," he said, "What's going on?"

I explained the situation, he gave me some reassuring words and prayed for us, and the conversation was over in ten minutes—but what a difference it made in my spiritual outlook! I stopped living in the undertow and started living in the overflow, and in time God brought us through the crisis in a wonderful way. I was so glad my friend was a benediction believer, even over the telephone.

We can be a blessing even with "snail mail." Yes, the Lord can see to it that a letter is delivered just when the recipient needs to read it. Of course, e-mail is the major messenger these days, so if the Lord prompts you to write, boot up and write!

Prayer is an absolute essential. On more than one occasion, my wife and I have both had the experience of waking up at night with a burden to pray for a specific friend or acquaintance. We didn't discover until days or weeks later that the person was in desperate need of prayer at that hour, and sometimes that friend was on the other side of the globe. God never worries about time zones.

Be a blessing at home, in your home church, and out in that needy world where everybody you meet is fighting a battle or carrying a burden. You cannot be everywhere, but you can serve right where you are. You may not bless everybody, but you can bless some. You cannot do everything, but you can do something. Like the little lad who gave his lunch to Jesus or like Peter, who loaned Him his boat, you can give what you have and the Lord will do the rest.

Blessed are the benediction believers, for they shall become more like Jesus as they share God's blessings with others!

THE MIZPAH PSEUDO-BENEDICTION

(GENESIS 31:49)

May the Lord keep watch between you and me when we are away from each other" (Genesis 31:49).

The Lord watch between me and thee, when we are absent one from another (KJV).

MANY YEARS AGO, this was a popular benediction among church groups. It was customary to stand and join hands, recite this passage as a benediction, and remain quiet for a moment before separating.

The words are beautiful—if you take them out of context. As my homiletics professors used to warn in seminary, "A text without a context is a pretext." That is exactly what the Mizpah "benediction" is—a pretext. It is a pseudo-benediction.

THE SETTING
FOR TWENTY YEARS, Jacob had been under the authority of his father-in-law Laban, and life had been miserable (see Genesis 31:38–42). Laban tricked Jacob into marrying his two daughters. He put him to work caring for his flocks and herds and did not treat him fairly. Jacob finally got up enough courage to take his family and flocks and escape from Laban and head back home to his own people. This was what God told him to do.

Of course Laban took off after Jacob, angry because his son-in-law had left secretly and had not given the family an opportunity for a going-away party. But the real cause of his anger was that somebody had stolen his household gods, and he wanted them back. Jacob admitted to leaving secretly, but he explained that he was afraid Laban would forbid his daughters to leave. Jacob could honestly say that he knew nothing about the missing idols. His favorite wife Rachel had them.

As he watched his tricky father-in-law rummage through all his personal baggage, Jacob became more and more angry, and twenty years of pent-up rage began to erupt. That is when he made his speech about all he had suffered, but Laban denied it and continued to make demands.

Once Jacob had expressed himself, he began to move toward achieving a truce and avoiding a family battle. The Lord had assured Jacob that He was with him (Genesis 31:1–3), so he had acted by faith in God's command. Jacob set up a large stone as a pillar and then asked everybody to pick up rocks and build a heap of stones next to the pillar. The pillar and the heap were to serve as a witness, a watchtower, and a boundary marker. The word *Mizpah* means "watchtower." The stones and the pillar bore witness that Jacob and Laban had reached an agreement that neither would cross this boundary to attack the other. But they were also reminders that the Lord Himself would be watching both men, so they had better behave themselves. If you want to express the agreement in poetry, try this.

> You don't trust me,
> And I don't trust you,
> But the Lord sees us both—
> So watch what out what you do!

Does that sound like a benediction? A better word would be *malediction*.

THE MEANING

JACOB WAS A GREAT man, but one of his weaknesses was his prone-
ness to scheme and not trust God to work things out. Instead of
just finding out God's will and doing it, Jacob tended to make his
own plans and ask God to bless them. Even though Jacob was the
second-born of the twins, it was God's plan that he be treated as
the firstborn and inherit both the birthright and the blessing. But
Jacob did not wait for God to work out His plan. He bought the
birthright from Esau and then deceived his father into giving him
the blessing. Because of this, Jacob had to flee from Esau, who had
threatened to kill him.

Jacob's twenty difficult years with Laban were a time of dis-
cipline from the hand of the Lord. Laban was also a schemer, so
Jacob had met his match. Sometimes the Lord disciplines us with
people just like ourselves. If we learn anything from Jacob's life,
it is that if two are to walk together, they must be in agreement
(Amos 3:3; 2 Corinthians 6:14–18). Jacob and Laban did not even
speak the same language (Genesis 31:47).

However, let's not be too hard on Jacob. He was a man of faith,
even if occasionally he did make his own plans. Jacob endured
twenty difficult years during which he and his wives built the house
of Israel. From Jacob on, the Old Testament is about the twelve
tribes of Israel. Were it not for those twelve men, God's purposes
on earth would not have been accomplished. God has deigned to
be called "the God of Jacob," and that is a compliment.

Let's also give Jacob credit for handling Laban's angry accusa-
tions with patience. Once Jacob had "told him off," Laban listened
to his son-in-law's wisdom and agreed to the truce. At least the two
families were able to sit down and eat together, which in the Near
East is the equivalent of a vow of friendship. Better to have a pillar
and a pile of stones than a cemetery with headstones!

We cannot use this experience as the basis for a Bible benediction, but Genesis 31 does assure us that the Lord is watching over

His own and fulfilling His purposes on this earth. When He is not permitted to rule, He overrules. "How unsearchable his judgments, and his paths beyond tracing out!"(Romans 11:33).

But please do not use Genesis 31:49 as a benediction.

Endnotes

1. Edwin S. Gausted, *Sworn on the Altar of God* (Grand Rapids: W. B. Eerdmans, 1996), 139.

2. *Notes on the Doctrine of God* (Boston: W. A. Wilde, 1948), 114.

3. *The Strong Name* (Edinburgh: T. & T. Clark, 1940), 253.

4. Stewart, *op. cit.,* 251.

5. Dietrich Bonhoeffer, *The Cost of Discipleship* (New York: Macmillan, 1963), 45, 47.

6. *New Seeds of Contemplation* (New York: New Directions, 1961), 194–95.

7. *The Metropolitan Tabernacle Pulpit* (Pilgrim Publications), vol. 23, 637.

8. *The New Testament in the Language of the People,* translated by Charles B. Williams (Chicago: Moody Press, 1996), 356.

9. *Metropolitan Tabernacle Pulpit,* vol. 32, 148.

10. Ruth Bell Graham, *Collected Poems: Footprints of a Pilgrim* (Grand Rapids, MI: Baker, 2002), 17. Used by permission.

11. *Firstborn* means "the highest, the sovereign," not "the first one to be raised." Jesus was raised never to die again, and because He lives, we have life. This is not true of any other person every resurrected.

Note to the Reader

The publisher invites you to share your response to the message of this book by writing Discovery House Publishers, Box 3566, Grand Rapids, MI 49501, USA. For information about other Discovery House books, music, or videos, contact us at the same address or call 1-800-653-8333. Find us on the Internet at http://www.dhp.org/ or send e-mail to books@dhp.org.